*Seventh Edition*

# American Industry
## Structure, Conduct, Performance

**Richard E. Caves**

*Harvard University*

**Prentice Hall,** *Englewood Cliffs, NJ 07632*

*Library of Congree Catalog-in-Publication Data*

Caves, Richard E.
    American Industry. structure, conduct, performance / Richard E.
Caves. -- 7th ed.
        p. cm. -- (Foundations of modern economics series)
    Includes bibliographical references and index.
        1. United States—Industries.    2. Industrial concentration —United
States.    3. Restraint of trade —United States.    I. Title.
II. Series.
HC106.5.C34    1992
338.0973--dc20                                                      91-21161
                                                                         CIP

PRENTICE-HALL FOUNDATIONS
OF MODERN ECONOMIC SERIES
Otto Eckstein, *Editor*

Acquisitions Editor: GARRET WHITE
Editorial/production supervision,
    interior design, and pagemakeup: ELIZABETH BEST
Copy editor: NANCY ANDREOLA
Prepress Buyer: TRUDI PISCIOTTI
Manufacturing Buyer: ROBERT ANDERSON
Editorial Assistant: DIANE DeCASTRO

© 1992, 1987, 1982, 1977, 1972, 1967, 1964
by Prentice-Hall Inc.
A Simon & Schuster Company
Englewood Cliffs, New Jersey 07632

Printed in the United States of America

10  9  8  7  6  5  4  3  2  1

ISBN 0-13-029893-X

Prentice-Hall International (UK) Limited, *London*
Prentice-Hall of Australia, Pty. Ltd., *Sydney*
Prentice-Hall of Canada, Ltd., *Toronto*
Prentice-Hall of Hispanoamericana, S.A., *Mexico*
Prentice-Hall of India Private Limited, *New Delhi*
Prentice-Hall of Japan, Inc., *Tokyo*
Simon & Schuster Asia Pte. Ltd., *Singapore*
Editora Prentice-Hall do Brasil, Ltda., *Rio de Janeiro*

# American Industry

## Structure, Conduct, Performance

# Contents

# Preface

This short textbook on industrial organization was originally written to provide a block for a modular introductory course on the principles of economics. Over the years it has come to find a number of niches beside the one for which it was originally intended. Some users employ it as the core of an undergraduate course on industrial organization, filling out the term with industry case studies or other collateral material. Some users employ it as a component of broader courses in programs on business administration or public policy. In successive revisions of the book I have sought to serve this rather diverse audience by sustaining a full coverage of the basic concepts and issues in industrial organization, updating the book in light of the subject's rapid development, giving it a slightly more "adult" tone, but leaving it accessible to students whose background in economics consists only of the microeconomic core of the principles course.

In this seventh edition the most substantial changes appear in Chapter 7 to reflect the major changes that have occurred in direct regulation in the United States and public enterprises elsewhere. A good deal of scholarly evidence on the effects of deregulation and privatization is now in hand, and it is now reported to the extent permitted by the volume's compact format. Other changes are numerous although minor, and appear throughout the book. An effort was made to update the blocks of illustrative material that provide textural variety.

The author is grateful to many users for their reactions, both general and specific, to the previous edition. A vote of thanks also goes to his own undergraduate students of industrial organization, who serve as guinea pigs for trying out new lines of exposition and pedagogical approaches.

R. E. C.

# American Industry
## Structure, Conduct, Performance

# Chapter 1

# The Business Sector
# and
# Its Organization

As you stroll the streets of New York, you will pass the headquarters of 42 of the nation's 500 largest industrial companies. You will also meet many sidewalk vendors of bagels, gelati, hot dogs, and umbrellas or sunglasses (depending on the weather). Between these Davids and Goliaths of American private enterprise lie 14 million incredibly diverse individual business units. They absorb the savings and labor services of the American populace. They ingest the nation's raw materials. They produce the vast stream of goods and services that we count as the gross national product.

## WHAT THIS BOOK IS ABOUT

Economists, studying the behavior and performance of the economic system, concern themselves with many features of these business units, for it is through the action of these hordes of individual firms that many of the general goals of the economy are gained or lost. Do they make the most efficient use of the nation's scarce factors of production? Do they produce the "best" combination of guns, butter, shoeshines, and the other goods and services desired by ultimate users? Do they contribute, within their ability, toward achieving a desirable rate of economic progress? Do they plan their activities in a way that helps stabilize national income and employment?

 Studying the behavior of all the individual business units in the nation at once amounts to nothing less than studying the whole economy. Studying them one by one, we promptly lose sight of the forest for the trees. The subject of "industrial organization" was conceived in an effort to split the difference between these two extremes. Individual business units come in contact with one another in *markets*. A market includes a group of buyers and sellers of a particular product engaged in setting the terms of sale of that product. The sellers participating in a given market are called collectively the *industry* producing that product. Much of this book deals with the ways in which the organization of these sellers affects the performance of the market and thus the nation's economic welfare. Therefore we use the term *industrial organization*.

A major branch of economics—price theory—deals with markets and industries. Hence, industrial organization, the investigation of real-life industries, is a form of applied price theory. This book shows you how to apply the basic concepts of price theory that you have learned to industries in the American economy. It summarizes what economists have discovered by applying these concepts to American industries. It reviews government policies toward business in the United States and illustrates how they should be evaluated and what changes might be considered.

## DO ENTERPRISES MAXIMIZE PROFITS?

Price theory rests heavily on the assumption that business firms act to maximize their profits. Of the various goals that might govern managers' decisions, the profit motive is strongest. Economists reason that managers in competitive industries *have* to try to maximize their profits. As they strive individually to succeed, they bring unconscious pressure to bear on any stragglers who are careless about their costs—that is, those who are not maximizing their profits. Those who fail to keep up with their more vigorous rivals suffer losses and sooner or later must drop from the race. But economists' theories about markets generally assume that managers aim to maximize their profits, even without the continuous pressure of perfect competition. Without this assumption, it is hard to predict how markets will behave.

In using price theory to study the actual behavior of businesses in the economy, we cannot avoid asking whether the assumption of profit maximization will furnish us with reliable predictions about business decisions. The business executive, like the rest of us, seeks to maximize personal utility. The business's profits are likely to be the main source of compensation, and thus of utility, for the executive. But what about the manager who sacrifices some profit for an easier life on the job or the glory of making "big deals"? If managers settled for some "acceptable" level of profit and then devoted their energies (and the business's resources) to other goals, economists would need to posit a different objective when they analyze business behavior. However, if managers strive chiefly for profits, with an occasional nod to other goals, then our analysis can safely focus on profit maximization as the prevailing goal.

## Profit Maximization and "Big Business"

When people question the role of profits in motivating business managers, they seldom have in mind your friendly neighborhood druggist. Because his profits *are* his income, he is not likely to let them languish. But the managers of giant corporations may have both the opportunity and the motive to pick goals other than profit maximization, if they choose.

They have the opportunity because they are not the owners of the giant businesses they run. Instead the owners—the holders of the company's equity shares—are thousands of individuals and financial institutions. In America's great corporations, the number of shareholders often considerably exceeds the number of employees. Many of these owners merely hold their shares and passively await the arrival of the dividend check. They have neither the time nor the resources to find out how well the management is running "their" company. Their only official votes in its affairs come at the annual stockholders' meeting. Rather than attend that, the great majority of them choose to sign proxies, which hand their votes over to the existing management. Even such large investors as mutual funds, pension funds, and other such financial institutions, which keep close tabs on management policies, usually take no active part in a company's affairs. Therefore the *control* of many large companies is said to be wrested from their owners and lodged in the hands of their managers. Management cannot ignore its shareholders' interests entirely. A "raider" could then corral enough shares, or shareholders' votes, to dump the existing management out in the street. This does happen, but it is not always a close threat.

Back in 1929, Adolf A. Berle and Gardiner C. Means reported on who controlled the largest 200 nonfinancial corporations in the United States, in the sense of holding the power to name their boards of directors. In only 22 companies did control rest in the hands of a cohesive majority shareholder group, and in 88 companies control had slipped entirely into the hands of management. Berle and Means suggested that, with no outside stockholder blocks exercising vigilance, the managers could control the board of directors, perpetuate themselves, and be the judges of their own success. Edward S. Herman reviewed Berle's and Means's findings and traced the rise of the "managerial" corporation through the twentieth century, starting with a sample of 40 large companies in 1900–1, proceeding to a revised version of the Berle-Means data, and providing a comparable analysis of the largest 200 in 1974. Even in 1900, 23.8 percent of the largest companies were under control of their managements, and this fraction grew to 40.5 percent in 1929 and 82.5 percent in 1974. The fraction controlled by majority owners slipped from 12.5 percent in 1900 to 9.5 percent in 1929 and 1.5 percent in 1974. In most of the remaining firms the largest stockholder commanded between 5 and 50 percent of the shares—enough to keep the managers on their toes though not enough to assure voting control over them. This trend stems from natural forces—the wider dispersion of share ownership, the dissipation of entrepreneurial family fortunes, and the sheer absolute sizes of the largest companies.[1] The same trend appears in other industrial countries, but is more advanced in the United States.

[1] Edward S. Herman, *Corporate Control, Corporate Power* (Cambridge, England: Cambridge University Press, 1981), Chap. 3.

## Other Goals for the Manager?

If corporate managements are no longer simply the hired hands of those who receive the firm's profits, should we expect that maximizing profits will remain their chief objective? Managers may gain utility from allocating their companies' resources in ways that diverge systematically from profit maximization.

*1. Size and growth.*    Managers might try to enlarge the company, maximizing its total revenue rather than its profit. Or they might speed its growth at the expense of profits.[2] The profit-maximizing management is not against growth, of course, but it sets the firm's growth at the best rate for the stockholders—the one that maximizes the present value of the profits that they expect to receive, taking the present and future together. Management might shoot for a growth rate faster than the one maximizing the present value of the shareholders' profits. The manager then enjoys the pleasures of making big discretionary choices over the direction of the firm's expansion. Utility, the hypothesis holds, comes from making big deals. Managers who are free of shareholders' control undertake more conglomerate mergers, which enlarge the firm but are not very likely to increase the shareholders' wealth.

*2. Risk avoidance.*    Managers might go for the quiet life. This could mean that they avoid risky projects that could turn out to be very profitable, settling instead for a smaller but more certain profit. John Kenneth Galbraith argued that the large corporation uses its resources to buy itself a secure environment, and we have some evidence that companies controlled by their managers are less willing to take chances on profitable actions that could bring new competitors onto the scene.[3]

*3. Perquisites.*    Managers might simply feather their own nests with high salaries and perquisites or inflated staffs of presentable helpers with nice manners. Indeed, managers' compensations apparently increase with their freedom from direct control by stockholders and with the monopoly power of their companies.[4] However, many companies tie their executives' salaries rather closely to the firm's profitability, and thus give them a strong incentive to maximize profits. For example, managers may receive stock options or pension rights that are closely tied to the long-run value of the company's shares; when the stockholders are well served, the price of the shares rises and the managers are rewarded accordingly.

What can we conclude from these possibilities? Are the giant corporations profit maximizers, or are they not? Economists have done many studies comparing the performance of companies under the cohesive control of their owners with companies whose control has fallen into their managers' hands. The results are not clear-cut, but there is some evidence that manager-controlled companies are less

[2]Robin Marris, "A Model of the 'Managerial' Enterprise," *Quarterly Journal of Economics*, Vol. LXXVII (May 1963), pp. 185–191.

[3]John Kenneth Galbraith, *The New Industrial State*, 4th ed. (Boston: Houghton Mifflin, 1985).

[4]Oliver E. Williamson, "Managerial Discretion and Business Behavior," *American Economic Review*, Vol. LIII (December 1963), pp. 1032–1057.

profitable. The avoidance of risks seems to play an important role in the managers' careers. Even when its outside owners exert significant control, a large company probably behaves in a risk-averse way. That is because risk-averse managers cannot "diversify" their jobs by working for 20 companies, whereas the risk-averse shareholder can easily own 20 companies' stocks.

Managerial behavior has recently become a subject of public debate; some observers assert that managers put too much weight on the long run by making their companies into "monuments" designed to last forever. The managers defend themselves, charging that the holders of corporate shares have lost sight of the long run, and in particular that money managers' lives revolve around corporate earnings in the current quarter, with little thought to anything beyond. Alas, it is not clear who wins this important debate.

### The Large Firm as a Bureaucracy

The large corporation is a bureaucracy. Like a government department or any other large organization employing many people, its managers must create chains of command and delegate the power to plan and carry out most decisions to people down the line. Some large companies, particularly those that make a wide range of distinct products, decentralize to the point that separate units make, advertise, and sell their own products. The firm's central management may retain close control of only a few functions, such as research and planning major investment projects.

Some scholars have decided that the question is not whether these organizations maximize profits but indeed whether they maximize anything at all! Top-management decisions take the form of setting and changing the "rules" that govern lesser decisions down the line, and of arbitrating when staff interests clash. Each staff or unit exerts its own pull on the decisions made by the corporation. The sales force may be eager for increased advertising to ease its way with potential customers. The production department may urge a cut in the number of different models produced in order to simplify control of the assembly lines. The treasurer's office may call for a price increase to improve the firm's cash position. The decisions that result might look more like a peace treaty among conflicting parties than a single-minded plan to maximize profits.

Nonetheless, the company does have a top management, and one of the manager's key responsibilities is to adjust the firm's organization chart and the balance of power among its interest groups, so that its bureaucracy casts up decisions conducive to its long-run survival and profitability. Study of the historical development of large American companies has shown how managers adapt the long-run strategies of their companies to changing threats and opportunities in the market place, altering their internal organizations so that employees are motivated to pull in the right direction and pay attention to the right things.[5] Such behavior looks very much like long-run profit maximization.

[5]Alfred D. Chandler, Jr., *Strategy and Structure: Chapters in the History of the American Industrial Enterprise* (Cambridge, MA: MIT Press, 1962).

Thus, despite the evident great differences between the "entrepreneur" of economic theory and the large business unit of modern life, they bear a family resemblance. The interest of big businesses in the tools of "scientific management," their stress on research aimed at cutting present costs and uncovering more valuable products for the future—these activities show the corporate manager busy with just the cost-cutting and profit-raising pursuits that economic theory ascribes to the independent entrepreneur. This behavior need not make the giant corporation more efficient—or less efficient—than the smaller, less bureaucratic firm run by its owner. But it does mean that we can use the assumption of profit maximization, and the body of price theory that economists have built on it, to guide our study of American industry—large and small firms together.

## INDUSTRIES IN THE ECONOMY

We defined an *industry* as the sellers of a particular product, one side of the *market* in which buyers and sellers arrange their transactions. The economist's concept of an industry corresponds to the way we speak of industries in everyday life. For instance, before World War II, the aluminum industry consisted of the Aluminum Company of America, the sole producer of aluminum ingots within the United States. American tariff walls kept out most imports, and other metals were not suitable substitutes for aluminum. Buyers in the market who wanted aluminum, and not any old metal, found that Alcoa was the "industry" from which they could buy it. The description of this market and industry posed no problem. Likewise, the many persons who wish on any particular day to buy or sell common shares of the American Telephone & Telegraph Co. all make their offers through a single center, the New York Stock Exchange. Again, the market and its participants are easy to identify.

### The Problem of Industry Boundaries

Just counting the heads of buyers and sellers participating in a product market does not, however, solve all the problems associated with labeling its sellers as a separate industry. Economic theory tells us that all participants in a market should be highly sensitive to the price prevailing in the market or to the deals offered by other transactors. And they should *not* be sensitive to conditions in other markets. The industries that we identify in the real world ought to satisfy this requirement. Herein arises the problem of *industry boundaries*—boundaries between products, boundaries in geographic space, and even boundaries in time.

For instance, as aluminum has grown more important among the key basic metals used in the modern economy, it has found itself in close rivalry with steel and other metals for more and more uses. Nowadays, a major price change in either the steel or the aluminum industry stirs some talk about a possible change in the other. Yet these parallel changes do not always occur, and many minor developments can happen in either industry without clearly affecting the other. That is, the buyers in the aluminum market are *very* sensitive to the price offers made by the aluminum industry; they are also *somewhat* sensitive to the price offers made by other metals producers. Where should the industry boundary be drawn—around the sellers of aluminum or around the sellers of basic metals? That is the problem of industry boundaries.

> Competition between industries was illustrated when the steel industry announced an 8 percent increase in tinplate prices, effective February 1, 1976. The makers of metal beverage cans began to switch massively from tinplate to aluminum, and the steel companies not only rescinded the increase but began giving discounts from the price they had previously charged. The steel makers apparently thought that the aluminum producers would follow their price increase, but competitive conditions in the aluminum industry at the time made a price rise out of the question.

A problem of industry boundaries can arise from buyers shifting from one group of sellers to another, as in the case just mentioned. It can also arise from sellers shifting their activities from one product to another. Producers weaving cotton fiber into cloth might easily be able to shift their looms to the weaving of linen or other fibers. In this case, the cotton weavers would be somewhat sensitive to developments in the linen industry. Should the industry boundary fall between cotton weavers and linen weavers or around the weaving industry?

Any attempt to classify all firms in the economy into separate industries obviously runs into thousands of boundary problems like these. Settling each one must be a matter of judgment. Drawing the boundaries too widely lumps together producers who are somewhat insensitive to one another's actions. Drawing them too narrowly places in separate industries firms that are actually quite sensitive to one another's actions. Published statistics for the United States and other major industrial countries usually allow a choice, identifying both a small number of widely defined industries and also a number of narrowly defined groups within each large industry. By fiddling with these statistics, one can usually draw a boundary among groups of sellers that will serve for the purpose at hand.

The other major problem of industry boundaries arises for products sold in regional markets, or in world markets that spill across national boundaries. Consider a product sold in regional markets. Beer consists—let's face it—mostly of water. Its transportation costs thus are quite high relative to the sale value of the product. In the United States a number of brands are advertised and sold nationally, but in each area they traditionally competed against a different group of local brands, which typically sold at a lower price and often held a large share of the local market. Should we consider breweries a national industry, or a group of interrelated regional industries? The problem calls for the same kind of judgment that is required in drawing the line between closely related products. The issue of local markets gets even more troublesome when we consider retail trade.

International trade and multinational companies demand that we stretch some industries' boundaries beyond those of the nation. The aluminum industry now includes about 50 independent companies worldwide, and prices in the United States and other industrial countries are closely tied together. A glance at any parking lot tells us that the automobile industry tilts toward worldwide status, even if national producers still enjoy the home team's advantage on their native turfs. In recent decades international trade has grown much faster than domestic production, for the United States and other industrial countries. So markets increasingly reach beyond the nation, and many large U.S. companies now count enterprises headquartered abroad among their chief rivals.

### Describing the Structure of an Industry

Once we have settled on an industry's boundaries, we turn to economic theory to tell us how the organization of its participants affects its performance. Economic theory provides a set of categories or market models which offer valuable guidance. You have learned that *monopoly* implies a single seller and *pure competition* a very large number of sellers within the relevant markets. *Monopolistic competition*, like pure competition, depends on a very large number of sellers occupying the market, even though each of them has some touches of individuality. *Oligopoly*, usually defined as "few" sellers occupying the market, covers everything else. (Since "few" includes all markets lying between "one" and "many," it surely has a large territory to itself.) Economic theory tells us that the differences between these market forms matter, because they affect the performance of the economy.

In order to relate these market models to actual markets in the American economy, we need some concepts for measuring the participants and their activities. For instance, an oligopoly of 3 sellers may behave very differently from one of 20 firms—unless, of course, 3 of the latter 20 have almost the whole market to themselves, with their 17 rivals subsisting on the fringe. We need a measurement tool that takes account of both the *number* and the *size distribution* of firms in a market, yet presents the result in a form simple enough that it is easy to interpret. The most widely used device is the *concentration ratio*. To compute a concentration ratio, you rank firms in order of size, starting from the largest in the industry. (Size is usually measured in terms of sales.) Then, starting from the top of the list, you add up the percentages for the top $x$ firms. Published statistics usually give concentration ratios for the largest 4, largest 8, and sometimes the largest 20 firms in an industry. The concentration ratio for a monopoly would, of course, be 100 percent; in a competitive industry the ratio for the largest 4 firms would have to be very small, perhaps 5 to 10 percent. The ratio for an oligopoly would lie between these limits. Table 1–1 gives concentration ratios for some selected United States industries in 1982. It also gives some idea of how industry boundaries are set according to the statistics collected by the federal government.

Two industries, *A* and *B*, both with 80 percent of their sales controlled by the largest four firms, might still differ in important ways. Industry *A* could embrace as few as five firms; if each of them held just 20 percent of the industry's sales, then the "largest four" would account for 80 percent. Industry *B* might have a very large number of firms accounting for the remaining 20 percent of sales. Likewise, the biggest firms might have a differing degree of dominance. The largest single firm in industry *A* might have as little as 20 percent of total sales; the leader in industry *B* might control as much as 50 or 60 percent. Figure 1–1 gives an example of how different

**TABLE 1–1**    Concentration Ratios in Selected American Manufacturing Industries, 1982

| Industry | Total Number of Companies | Percentage of Value of Shipments Accounted for by: Largest 4 | Largest 8 | Largest 20 |
|---|---|---|---|---|
| Chewing gum | 9 | 95 | 99+ | 100 |
| Motor vehicles and car bodies | 284 | 92 | 97 | 99 |
| Electric lamps | 113 | 91 | 96 | 98 |
| Flat glass | 49 | 85 | 99+ | 99+ |
| Turbines and turbine generators | 71 | 84 | 92 | 96 |
| Malt beverages | 67 | 77 | 94 | 99 |
| Carbon black | 8 | 73 | 100 | 100 |
| Sewing machines | 86 | 71 | 82 | 93 |
| Primary aluminum | 15 | 64 | 88 | 100 |
| Soaps and detergents | 642 | 60 | 79 | 83 |
| Cookies and crackers | 296 | 59 | 71 | 85 |
| Radio and TV receiving sets | 432 | 49 | 70 | 86 |
| Macaroni, spaghetti | 208 | 42 | 68 | 85 |
| Pens and mechanical pencils | 129 | 41 | 62 | 81 |
| Envelopes | 196 | 28 | 46 | 67 |
| Women's and misses' dresses | 5489 | 6 | 10 | 17 |

*Source*: U.S. Bureau of the Census, 1982 *Census of Manufactures, Concentration Ratios in Manufacturing*, MC82–S–7 (Washington, DC, 1986), Table 5.

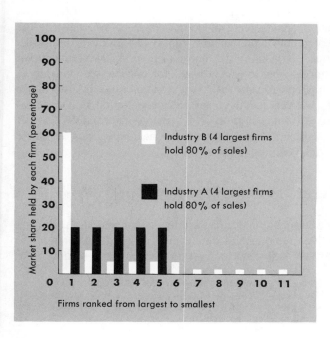

Firms ranked from largest to smallest

**FIGURE 1–1**  Possible differences in number and size distribution of firms between industries with identical concentration ratios.

these industries might look. Despite these problems, the concentration ratios for different industries usually give a fairly accurate picture of where they stand comparatively in the spectrum running from pure competition to "pure" monopoly. This is because, as a matter of fact, most industries have some large and some small firms in them. One Gulliver surrounded by a crowd of Lilliputians (industry $B$) is uncommon; so is a clump of equally giant Brobdingnagians (industry $A$). Still, concentration levels cannot be compared easily. Which industry is more concentrated, malt beverages (higher four-firm concentration) or carbon black (higher eight-firm concentration and fewer firms)?

Another important qualification for interpreting concentration ratios is the role of foreign trade, pushing market boundaries beyond the nation. Concentration ratios are calculated from shipments by domestic *producers*. If the United States is a meaningful market at all, we really need data on the concentration of *sellers*. Table 1–1 shows that the largest four sewing machine producers account for 71 percent of U.S. producers' shipments; but imports were as large as U.S. production, so seller concentration must be much lower. In the automobile industry, for example, four-firm producer concentration was 100 percent in 1977 but four-firm seller concentration only 86 percent.[6] Another complication arises from U.S. exports, counted in total shipments but not reaching U.S. customers. If the larger producers export proportionally more of their output than small ones (a pattern commonly observed), another upward bias is built into producer concentration ratios.

A lot of the discussion of industry types in this book will run in terms of concentration ratios. We will often find it easier to talk about "more concentrated" or "less concentrated" industries than about the separate types of industries described in economic theory, such as "purely competitive" or "oligopolistic." This does not mean that we are dropping these theoretical models. We shall use the theories of monopoly and oligopoly to predict how "highly concentrated" industries are likely to behave. We shall depend on the theory of monopolistic competition and pure competition to tell us what to expect from "unconcentrated" industries. Switching over to describing industries by their concentration ratios has two major advantages, however: (1) we can readily measure concentration in the actual industries around us; and (2) concentration is a "continuous variable," and it reminds us that actual industries do not fall into a few neat categories but range continuously in concentration from top to bottom.

## SELLER CONCENTRATION IN THE AMERICAN ECONOMY

Because of the significance that economic theory ascribes to concentration, we need a general idea of the relative importance of the different market structures in the American economy. Published statistics provide a rather complete picture of the

---

[6]William James Adams, "Producer-Concentration as a Proxy for Seller-Concentration: Some Evidence from the World Automotive Industry," *Journal of Industrial Economics*, Vol. XXIX (December 1980), pp. 185–202. The discrepancy is more marked for smaller economies; in the Netherlands two-firm producer concentration was 100, two-firm seller concentration 26.

manufacturing sector, where about one-quarter of the country's national income originates, but estimates for the rest of the American economy must be pieced together from diverse sources. William G. Shepherd summarized the level and trend of concentration by classifying each U.S. industry into one of four categories: monopoly, dominant firm (a leader holding 50 to 90 percent of the market), tight oligopoly (four-firm concentration above 60 percent), and effective competition (the rest).[7] His classifications took into account market-definition problems, international competition, and the presence of anticompetitive regulation in some sectors. He also "peeked" at the behavior patterns of industries to confirm the diagnoses offered by the concentration statistics. Furthermore, his classification covered three years, 1939, 1958, and 1980, in order to reveal the long-run trend in competitiveness. His results are summarized in Figure 1–2, which shows the changing distribution of sectors among his four categories. Shepherd found that national income originating in the effectively competitive sectors had increased by half in over four decades, from 52.4 to 76.7 percent of the total. Put another way, markets that do not seem effectively competitive shrank from about one-half to about one-quarter of the economy. Only a small part of the trend toward greater competitiveness was due to declining concentration of domestic producers. Much more important, Shepherd felt, were the increase in international competition (lower trade barriers, greater strength of other industrial economies) and the results of public policy (antitrust laws, removal of protective regulation).

**FIGURE 1–2**    Trend in distribution of market structures in the U.S. economy, 1939–1980.

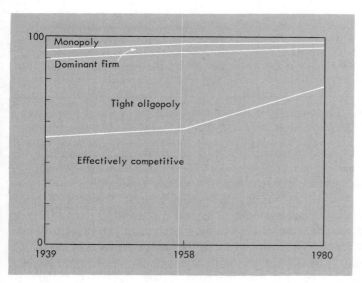

For the manufacturing sector, we have accurate data on both the nominal concentration of domestic producers and their effective concentration after each industry's concentration ratio has been corrected for errors in market definition. These errors arise because definitions of industries used by the Bureau of the Census diverge from economic markets in either geographical area (regional or local market; international competition) or product coverage (substitutes in other industries omitted; noncompeting goods included). Table 1–2 shows the distribution of concentration ratios in manufacturing for the year 1977, with and without these corrections. Although the corrections for some industries are very large, the overall distribution does not change much. The corrected ratios do tend to squeeze into the moderately concentrated segment of the distribution: most industries that are highly concentrated according to the Census Bureau's figures face some import competition, while many of its unconcentrated industries are regional or too broadly defined.

**TABLE 1–2**    Concentration of U.S. Manufacturing Industries, 1977, with and without Adjustments to Correct Market Misdefinitions

| Percentage of Shipments Made by Largest Four Firms | Number of Industries | |
|---|---|---|
| | Census Definitions of Industries | Corrected for Market Boundaries |
| 91-100 | 2 | 1 |
| 81-90 | 12 | 8 |
| 71-80 | 15 | 22 |
| 61-70 | 24 | 27 |
| 51-60 | 42 | 40 |
| 41-50 | 53 | 66 |
| 31-40 | 76 | 96 |
| 21-30 | 90 | 86 |
| 11-20 | 78 | 52 |
| 0-10 | 21 | 15 |

Source: Data provided by Leonard W. Weiss and George Pascoe, updating their Adjusted Concentration Ratios in Manufacturing —1972. Federal Trade Commission (n.d.).

What about concentration in other parts of the economy? Published statistics are sketchy, but the general patterns show through clearly. Public utilities, which are regulated by various agencies of federal and state governments, operate partly under conditions of local monopoly or very high seller concentration. The local telephone company or electric utility holds a monopoly of its service in almost all cases—for good reason, as we shall see in a moment. The market for transportation of persons and goods is "local" in the same sense. The customer shops for transportation from Pittsburgh to Miami—not just for a thousand-mile trip in any direction. The relevant markets for transportation services between particular pairs of cities are quite concentrated, yet in the case of airlines and highway trucking (but not railroads) sellers can readily move in or out of the market. (As we shall see in Chapter 2, they contrast sharply to many markets in which new entrants face substantial disadvantages.) Therefore, these markets for the most part are effectively competitive.

Many of the industries that produce primary raw materials are fairly unconcentrated. Agriculture is the classic example of the purely competitive industry. Not only are there 2.2 million farms in the country, but each individual crop or product is grown on a relatively large number of them. In a few cases, such as lemons and peaches in California, the growers have banded together in cooperative organizations that act as monopolistic sellers. And, of course, government price-support programs strongly affect some crops. But the fact remains that many small sellers occupy the market. This also holds true for forest products. The mining sectors of the economy vary greatly in concentration. Some, such as coal, contain numerous producers. Others are more concentrated, but international sellers of many primary products keep their prices in line with world markets. At times worldwide concentration or cartels have given producers in these sectors real monopoly clout; the Organization of Petroleum Exporting Countries (OPEC) is a prime example.

Many firms operate in the construction sector, making small-scale and nonspecialized forms of construction competitive. Concentration is importantly higher, however, in some specialized and large-scale forms and in some local markets. Retail stores and most service industries—from banks to barber shops—sell in limited local markets. The national totals for any of these portions of the economy show many thousands of small units, but some of them located in isolated areas may enjoy something like local monopolies—the only hardware or furniture store in a small town, for example. Even in a big city, some distance often separates different stores or service establishments of the same kind. One unit may possess some monopoly power over customers who dislike struggling through traffic jams to make contact with a rival.

### Trends in Seller Concentration

Has seller concentration been increasing? Every so often the fear is voiced that big businesses will swallow or drive out small ones, and that a few giant firms will come to dominate the economy. What are the facts? In the manufacturing sector we know that concentration rose rapidly in the late nineteenth century, that famous era of the trusts. Since the turn of the century, concentration has followed no sustained trend upward or downward. Professor G. Warren Nutter's archaeological labors disclose that around 1900, 32.9 percent of value added in manufacturing came from industries whose four largest firms accounted for 50 percent or more of output.[8] The corresponding figure for 1963 was 33.1 percent. The average level of concentration does not always stay stuck as tightly as these figures suggest, however. It dropped sharply during World

---

[8]G. Warren Nutter and H. A. Einhorn, *Enterprise Monopoly in the United States* (New York: Columbia University Press, 1969), Chaps. 1–3.

War II, then drifted back upward. Between 1947 and 1972 the average concentration ratio (weighted by industries' value added) rose from 35.3 to 39.2, but it has drifted downward a bit since 1972.[9]

People do not confine their worries to concentration in particular industrial markets. They often express concern over the dominance of "big business" in the general economy, apart from monopoly in particular markets. In Chapter 3 we shall examine the dominance of the large corporation, its causes and consequences.

## STUDYING INDUSTRIAL ORGANIZATION

Why all this concern with "seller concentration"? Why do economists stress this descriptive trait of an industry, above all others? Why should this feature seem so much more important than, say, whether the industry makes goods for consumers or for other businesses, or whether or not its demand varies with the seasons?

The answer is that we believe that seller concentration affects an industry's social performance—its contribution to the general economic welfare—in a vital way. Economic theory concludes that industries with high seller concentration— monopolies—are likely to charge higher prices and earn higher profits than industries with low concentration—competitive industries. We object to this uneven distribution of profits because it signals a defect in the distribution of the nation's factors of production between the two kinds of industries. Monopolies gain their excess profits by consciously restricting output. Monopolies employ too few of the nation's resources, or, to turn the proposition around, competitive industries employ too many. If we switched some resources from competitive to monopolized industries, the value of society's output to consumers would increase, and our stock of scarce resources would be more effectively used.

This proposition about high concentration leading to incorrect resource allocation is a *hypothesis* of economic theory. It predicts the pattern of profits that we might find in real-life industries. It tells us something of the significance of this pattern for economic welfare. Such hypotheses are the stock-in-trade of industrial organization. As in any other scientific inquiry, a hypothesis at the start is nothing but an educated guess. Before a hypothesis receives a seal of approval, it has to be tested somehow—by showing that it furnishes reliable predictions about the facts. Thus, the study of industrial organization does not stop with spinning out such hypotheses and arranging them in artful fashion. It also tests them, wherever factual information will permit, against actual experience.

One swallow does not make a summer, and one hypothesis about seller concentration does not provide enough grist for a whole branch of economics. We shall encounter many more of them, taking the same form but including different variables, in the following pages. In order to organize them efficiently, we need a simple framework of concepts. These concepts should allow us to translate into

[9]For a survey of the evidence, see F. M. Scherer and David Ross, *Industrial Market Structure and Economic Performance*, 3rd ed. (Boston: Houghton Mifflin, 1990), Chap. 3.

practical terms the many specific models of markets that are provided by economic theory, and to keep the empirical content of these models close at hand. A theorist can say, "I assume $X$." The applied economist studying industries must be prepared for $X$, $Y$, or $Z$ as they come along. Nobody can think about every influence at once, but the applied economist—or the business manager—must be ready to assess the effect of each of many influences on an industry's performance.

The most popular framework used for this purpose turns on three simple concepts—market structure, market conduct, and market performance. *Market structure* consists of the relatively stable features of the market environment that influence the rivalry among the buyers and sellers operating within it. *Market conduct* consists of the policies that participants adopt toward the market (and their rivals in it) with regard to their price, the characteristics of their product, and other terms that influence market transactions. *Market performance* is our normative appraisal of the social quality of the allocation of resources that results from a market's conduct.

The economic theorist says that monopolies tend to earn excess profits. The industrial-organization economist says that market structures marked by high seller concentration tend to exhibit allocative inefficiency, a form of poor market performance. The two statements are equivalent, but the industrial-organization economist is also keeping in mind that market structure includes many elements other than seller concentration that can affect allocative efficiency and profits. Indeed, seller concentration may even not be the most important of them. (We consider these other elements of structure in Chapter 2.)

The concepts of market structure, conduct, and performance thus serve as useful main headings for our intellectual filing system. But they do much more than that—they embody the key causal hypotheses of economic theory. Theory tells us that market structure (the environment) determines market conduct (the behavior of economic agents within that environment) and thereby sets the level of market performance. Working backward, if we are concerned with some dimension of market performance, our trinity of concepts offers us an inventory of the aspects of market behavior and the elements of market structure that might determine how well a market performs in that dimension.

If we can uncover reliable links between elements of structure and elements of performance, we have a powerful tool for economic analysis and policy. We can predict the performance of any industry in which we are interested. Even more important, public policy can sometimes be used to change the elements of market structure or modify patterns of conduct. If we can spot some features of market structure or conduct that regularly cause poor market performance, we may find the key to designing policies to change the environment and raise the level of performance.

Economists who use the structure-conduct-performance framework disagree in the emphases that they give to its elements. Some would give market structure and market conduct "equal time" as determinants of performance. Others take the view that conduct (except for random elements) is largely determined by structure; hence market performance depends heavily on market structure, and we need pay rather little attention to the behavior that links the two. Still others urge that some kinds of conduct demand close attention because they can cause market structure to change.

The rest of this book will be organized around the concepts of structure, conduct, and performance. We have already examined the most familiar of the elements of market structure—seller concentration. In Chapter 2 we consider others. Chapter 3 takes up as an element of market structure the large firm that overspills its principal market and operates in many other markets. Chapter 4 outlines the types of market conduct. In Chapter 5 we define the dimensions of market performance and review the evidence that connects them to their determinants in structure and conduct. Chapters 6 and 7 survey public policies designed to secure improved market performance.

## SUMMARY

The subject of "industrial organization" applies the economist's models of price theory to the industries in the world around us. It aims to increase our understanding of how these industries operate and to appraise their contribution to economic welfare. It also helps us to appraise government policy toward business. Price theory builds its deductions on the assumption that business managers seek to maximize their profits. Business motives in the real world are much more complex, but this assumption still provides a good starting point.

Defining "industries" in the real world entails some tricky problems of judgment, because buyers and sellers can often shift easily from one product to another, and because some products are sold in regional or world rather than national markets. Once we have drawn an industry's boundaries, we can use the concept of "seller concentration" to measure the number and size distribution of its member firms. Identifying an industry's structure with its level of concentration provides a useful parallel with, and partial substitute for, the theoretical categories of monopoly, oligopoly, monopolistic competition, and pure competition. Data on the U.S. economy reveal that situations of oligopoly (high or moderate concentration) are fairly common in the manufacturing sector and occur here and there elsewhere in the economy. The concentration of domestic producers has shown little change over the years in most industries. Nonetheless, effective competition has apparently increased in the past half-century because of increased rivalry through international trade as well as certain public policies.

Seller concentration is one element of market structure. We organize the study of industrial organization around the concepts of market structure, market conduct, and market performance. Economic theory tells us that market performance is determined by market structure and conduct, although their relative importance remains subject to debate.

# Chapter 2

# Elements
# of Market Structure

We defined the concentration ratio as a measure of the extent to which the larger sellers control the bulk of the industry's sales. Concentration is merely one element of *market structure*, the economically significant features of a market that affect the behavior of firms in the industry supplying that market.

## RELATIONS AMONG STRUCTURAL ELEMENTS

The main elements of market structure are as follows:

1. Seller concentration.
2. Product differentiation.
3. Barriers to the entry of new firms.
4. Buyer concentration.
5. Height of sunk costs and barriers to exit.
6. Growth rate of market demand.
7. Import competition.

It is not easy to rank these elements in importance, but everybody's list would include the first three near the top. We will concentrate on product differentiation and barriers to entry in this chapter but also give some attention to the last four items on the list.

What does determine the importance of these elements? Economic theory tells us that concentrated industries are likely to perform poorly, employing too few factors of production and channeling too many into less concentrated industries. In Chapter 5 we shall develop other hypotheses about the effect of high concentration on performance. The other elements of market structure share this power to influence market performance. The important elements of structure are the ones that can and do make a major difference for market performance. Whether they *can* influence performance is a question for economic theory. Whether they actually *do* wield a potent and regular influence can be settled only by empirical research. Our list of key elements of market structure rests on the judgment that its items meet these two tests.

To count as significant, an element of market structure must show other properties as well. It must be both observable and measurable. Its value should tend to change little over time (otherwise, it could hardly be a stable influence on conduct). It should be, by and large, independent of the policy choices made by firms in the industry. (If firms can change their structural environment, it is hardly a stable influence on their behavior.)

### What Determines Concentration?

Another test for a significant element of market structure is whether it is independent of the other elements. Does it really stand as a separate influence, or does it rest on more fundamental prime causes? We can raise this question about seller concentration. Why should the automobile industry include only a few firms, while thousands make wooden kitchen cabinets? Is it a matter of chance or of historical happenstance? Are industries concentrated because at some time the "bad guys" drove their rivals to the wall, whereas in unconcentrated industries the "good guys" never got around to it? Or does seller concentration itself rest on some stable forces which we can locate among the other elements of market structure?

After we have looked at such factors as barriers to entry and product differentiation, we shall indeed conclude that concentration by and large rests on and reflects other elements of market structure. Even before getting to that stage, we can easily convince ourselves that the level of concentration in the typical industry stems not just from chance factors. Suppose for a moment that it were all an accident. Then, the same industry observed in *different countries* would probably exhibit varying market structures. If the aluminum industry were monopolized in the United States, it might include a hundred firms in Canada and a thousand firms in the United Kingdom on a random basis. Is this actually the case, or can we safely assume that an industry that is highly concentrated in one advanced economy will probably be highly concentrated in another? Table 2–1 ranks a dozen closely matched industries by their concentration in the United States and shows their rankings in four other industrial countries. The rankings are certainly not identical, but they do bear a family resemblance. Cigarettes are at or near the top, shoes the bottom, for all countries. As we identify the other key elements of market structure, some reasons for these similar rankings will become apparent.[1]

---

[1]Differences between countries help to explain some of the discrepancies in rankings found in Table 2–1. Cement, a regional industry, is less concentrated in far-flung countries like the United States and Canada. Concentration tends to be low when a country's market is particularly large—the German brewing industry is an example.

**TABLE 2–1**    Range of Selected Industries in Order of Decreasing Seller Concentration in Five Countries, 1970

| Industry | United States | United Kingdom | West Germany | France | Canada |
|---|---|---|---|---|---|
| Cigarettes | 1 | 1 | 1 | 1 | 2 |
| Glass bottles | 2 | 6 | 2 | 4 | 1 |
| Refrigerators | 3 | 7 | 5 | 1 | 6 |
| Storage batteries | 4 | 5 | 4 | 3 | 7 |
| Antifriction bearings | 5 | 3 | 3 | 7 | 3 |
| Ordinary steel | 6 | 10 | 6 | 4 | 5 |
| Brewing | 7 | 8 | 11 | 8 | 3 |
| Fabric weaving | 8 | 11 | 12 | 10 | 8 |
| Paints | 9 | 9 | 9 | 11 | 11 |
| Petroleum refining | 10 | 4 | 8 | 9 | 10 |
| Cement | 11 | 2 | 7 | 6 | 9 |
| Shoes | 12 | 12 | 10 | 12 | 12 |

*Source*: Based on F.M. Scherer and others, *The Economics of Multi-Plant Operation: An International Comparisons Study* (Cambridge, MA: Harvard University Press, 1975), pp. 426–428.

## PRODUCT DIFFERENTIATION

The first of these additional traits of market structure that we need to consider goes by the awkward name of *product differentiation*. To get at its meaning, consider an industry where it is absent. When North Dakota wheat growers send their crops to market, one farm's wheat is not different physically from its neighbor's. The buyer has no basis for forming any preference between them. Indeed, the buyer cannot even tell one output from the other, and would never pay a cent more a bushel for one farmer's wheat than for that of another. If one farm asked more than the going market price for the crop, it would sell none. Even if a new secret ingredient were claimed the experienced commercial buyer could tell otherwise and would refuse to pay more than the going price.

In few markets is the product perfectly "undifferentiated" in this way. Usually a product has some distinguishing marks that make the brand sold by one producer not quite the same as a competitor's. The word *brand* itself is a tip-off. As soon as we can recognize one producer's output and distinguish it from another's, they are no longer undifferentiated. Furthermore, behind the packaging or brand mark, all sorts of differences may exist. Two toothpastes may differ in flavor; two detergents, in the amount of suds they produce. When we come to durable goods, the possibilities for differentiation become enormous. Two makes of automobiles can differ in steering, suspension, and in thousands of other ways, including stylistic features.

Brands of a product can also be differentiated in ways not built into the product itself. The "conditions of sale" can differ in many ways, particularly if the producing firm controls the retail outlets through which its products reach customers. The service provided and terms of the guarantee also can differentiate brands of a product. Even different locations at which branded goods are sold may differentiate them.

The importance of these types of differentiation lies in their effect on consumers' demand for the product. Each customer is likely to have some definite preferences among the available brands of a commodity. One may feel that soap *A* does more for his or her complexion or personal magnetism. Another may favor soap *B*. This trait of the demand for soap potentially has a vital effect on the market behavior of the soap manufacturers. Therefore, whereas the North Dakota wheat farmer who raises the price above the going market level will sell no wheat, the manufacturer of soap *A* who sets a price above what others charge will still keep those customers who think that soap *A* has especially attractive properties. By the same token, if the manufacturer of soap *A* cuts its price below the market level, the firm may not suddenly find itself deluged with customers. Some will be on the verge of switching to brand *A*, and a modest price cut will swing them over. Others, however, will stick with other brands that have a special attraction to them.

Differentiation greatly expands the market strategies open to the producer. As Figure 2–1 shows, it makes the firm's demand curve less elastic. In reacting to whatever changes in market conditions may come along, it has less incentive to reduce prices and more incentive to increase them. The firm's strategic options also expand, because it can now react to changing market conditions by changing the traits of the product as well as its price. The size (and character) of the firm's advertising and similar sales-promotion efforts also become instruments of competition.

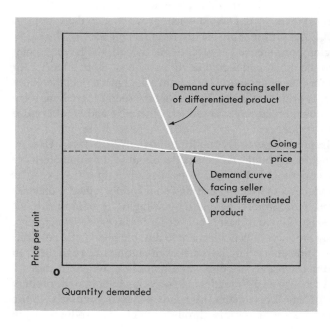

**FIGURE 2–1** Demand curves facing individual sellers of differentiated and undifferentiated products.

Demand curve facing seller of differentiated product

Going

price

Demand curve facing seller of undifferentiated product

Price per unit

O

Quantity demanded

If a seller spends money on advertising, then it is very likely that it sells a differentiated product. This holds true almost by definition, since an undifferentiated product *is* one whose consumers cannot perceive any differences among brands. Growers of many kinds of fruits find that it does not pay to advertise the product of their own orchards under a brand name. But they often do band together and advertise their crop cooperatively. The Sunkist brand is an example. They may be able to swing consumers' preferences away from grapefruit to lemons, but one lemon continues to look about like another, no matter what anybody says.

### Importance of Product Differentiation

How prevalent and important is product differentiation in the American economy? Products whose physical units cannot be told apart (such as wheat or steel) will tend to be largely undifferentiated in the market place. Even where physical differences exist, no economic differentiation may arise if the buyers can make an exact appraisal of the differences *and* if every buyer makes the same appraisal. For instance, coal of different grades and from different regions may vary in energy content and in the quantities and types of impurities contained in it. Major users of coal, however, such as giant electrical utilities, can readily measure these differences. They may decide that type $A$ coal has exactly 1.3 times the energy value to them per ton as type $B$ coal. And then they will be willing to pay more for type $A$ than type $B$. But this is not the same as product differentiation. The utilities will pay more for type $A$, but only 1.3 times the price per ton of $B$, and not a penny more. Even homogeneous physical goods, however, sometimes get differentiated a bit by the seller's reputation for reliable delivery or by the auxiliary services provided.

Differentiation really takes hold where products are complicated or where buyers' tastes are diverse. Take a complex product such as a camera. It has many different attributes—type of picture taken, simplicity, durability, automatic features, size and weight, and so on. Each buyer has preferences about these and many other features. Because we all have different preferences, each auto maker tends to offer different combinations of features, and cars become differentiated goods. Other goods, such as headache remedies and cigarettes, seem to be differentiated even though their physical traits vary little from one brand to the next. We all have preferences about brands of beer, yet only the rare quaffer can identify his favorite brew in a blind test! For these products, differentiation arises because the utility one gets from consuming the product is ill-defined (did it cure your headache or did your headache simply go away when you stopped reading this book?) or because it depends on how we think others will respond to our choices (how will *she* respond to my after-shave lotion?). Some goods, therefore, are differentiated because of the social context of their consumption or because "objective" information has little relevance or value for guiding buyers' choices.[2]

[2] R. E. Caves and P. J. Williamson, "What Is Product Differentiation, Really?" *Journal of Industrial Economics*, Vol. XXXIV (December 1985), pp. 113–132.

Consider the automobile as a highly differentiated product combining all these features of consumer preferences. It can satisfy a wide range of wants: reliability, economy of operation, speed, prestige, and so on. Individual households buy a new car only occasionally, and thus have little direct experience. More objective evidence can be obtained to guide their choices but it is costly. A particular make of automobile can offer the different features which owners seek in widely varying combinations. Furthermore, the industry's own policies help to increase the amount of differentiation which would occur naturally. Heavy advertising is one. Another is periodic model changes. Still another is maintaining franchised dealers, who advertise and promote particular makes of cars locally and provide specialized servicing, which boosts the differentiation still further.

From these considerations we can designate the sectors of the American economy in which product differentiation is likely to be important. As just suggested most manufacturing industries that sell to other producers are nearly free of differentiation. The exceptions to this rule are industries that offer complex goods (machinery, for example) and goods that interact in complex ways with the producer-buyer's own production process (such as parts that must fit with very close tolerances). In the consumer-goods sector, durables are all differentiated by their complex attributes and the diverse "bundles" of these attributes that producers typically offer. Simple consumer goods include both undifferentiated ones (lettuce) and those that are differentiated by "image" and interpersonal elements of taste. Outside of the manufacturing sector, local retail and service trades usually show significant differentiation based on location and qualities of service. Contract construction and some finance industries provide undifferentiated exceptions, but the differentiating personality of "your neighborhood druggist" is the general rule in the service and retail-trade sectors.

## BARRIERS TO ENTRY

We have seen how concentration and product differentiation furnish important elements of an industry's market structure. Both count as major features of the economic environment of the firm. Both effectively determine the kinds of actions firms might take in their search for profits. Thus, both help to predict how firms in an industry are likely to behave.

### Barriers to Entry as a Structural Trait

Barriers to entry comprise another major segment of the firm's economic environment. Just as concentration reflects the number of *actual* market rivals of a firm, so the condition of entry tells the story about *potential* rivals. To see the potential importance of the condition of entry, imagine a monopoly firm that has no actual rivals but knows full well that raising its price above the level that yields normal profits will draw a horde of rivals into competition. To preserve a quiet life, it may choose to set a "competitive" price, earning no excess profits but attracting no rivals. In this case, we would say that entry is "easy." New firms can produce at costs no higher than those of the going firm. This "monopolist" has no long-run monopoly power at all.

Take the opposite case—a monopoly that controls patents that protect it completely from rivals, actual or potential. We can say that entry is "blockaded," and the monopolist's position becomes perfectly protected. The monopoly can charge whatever price will maximize its profits in the short run, and still retain the entire market in splendid isolation in the long run.

### Measuring Barriers to Entry

These two cases, easy entry and blockaded entry, suggest a way of looking at the condition of entry as a feature of market structure. In the latter case, the monopoly can charge as much for its product as the price that will maximize its short-run profits, and still attract no rivals. In the former case, any price higher than that which yields a normal return on its capital (that is, no monopoly profits) attracts entry. Then we can think of an industry's barriers to entry as measured in principle by *the highest price that will just fail to tempt new firms into the industry.*

Figure 2–2 gives a more specific interpretation to these ideas. It shows average *(AC)* and marginal *(MC)* cost curves for a monopolistic producer, along with the demand *(D)* and marginal revenue *(MR)* curves that it faces. It would gain maximum short-run profits by setting price $P_m$, which results from offering that quantity of output for which marginal cost equals marginal revenue. We can also identify a "competitive price," $P_c$. Like the price prevailing in a perfectly competitive industry, it is equal to both marginal and average costs. The

**FIGURE 2–2**   Measurement of barriers to entry.

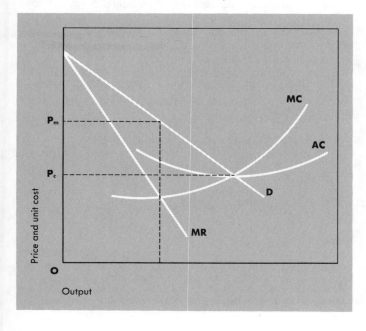

competitive price would yield just enough profit to keep the firm in the business.[3] Now we can measure the condition of entry. "Low" barriers to entry will permit a price not much above $P_c$, if rivals are not to be tempted into the industry. "High" barriers to entry, on the other hand, will permit a price at or near that which maximizes short-run profits without attracting new competitors. In between high and low barriers, we can locate moderate barriers to entry, allowing a price yielding some profit above and beyond the competitive level, but not the short-run monopoly maximum.

### Scale-Economy Barriers to Entry

Why should a new firm be at a disadvantage compared to one already in the industry? The preceding example mentioned one possible cause: control of patent rights by the established firm. Many other factors help to explain why the going firm might have an advantage. The many causes that come to mind fall into three analytical categories.

*Scale-economy* barriers to entry arise when firms do not achieve the lowest possible costs until they have grown to occupy a large share of the market. Figure 2–3 offers an illustration. It shows the average unit cost curve of any firm, new or old, in some industry. (Its shape may look strange to you. Rather than having the usual textbook U-shape, it shows costs falling at first and then constant over a very large range of outputs; this, however, is how economic research suggests that long-run cost curves for firms most commonly look.) The firm would enjoy economies of scale as it grows from any very small output toward output *OB*, for average unit costs decline over this range. Now, suppose

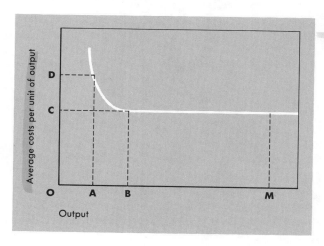

**FIGURE 2–3**  Entry barriers due to scale economies.

---

[3]The student who learned price theory well will note that the demand curve in Figure 2–2 need not pass through the point where the marginal cost curve intersects the average cost curve. Equality of price and average cost (including normal profits) is the essential idea of "competitive price" here.

that output $OB$ would supply a large share of the market. Let output $OM$, which is three times output $OB$, equal total sales in the market at the going price.

Consider the dilemma that faces any new firm entering this industry. Three existing firms, each producing $OB$, can supply the entire market. If the newcomer also builds a plant big enough to achieve the available scale economies, $OB$, it has to wrest from the existing firms a substantial part of their market. To sell as much as they do, on the average, it would have to cut each of them back from a third to a fourth of the national market. Both entrant and incumbents may find themselves running losses.

The newcomer has another alternative, but one that may prove no more attractive. It can build a small plant, with a capacity such as $OA$, and sell its whole output without making a sizable dent in the market of the going firms. But it must pay the penalty of inefficiency due to small scale. In Figure 2–3, a firm producing output $OA$, half the output $OB$ which just gains all the available scale economies, incurs costs half again as high as the larger firm. Either way, the new firm faces disadvantages that the older rivals avoid.

This two-horned dilemma that scale economies pose for the newcomer also tells us how to discover whether scale economies create a high or low barrier to entry in a given industry. The greater the output of a single firm that has gained all scale economies relative to the market, the harder it is for a new firm to start out at an "efficient" size. (In terms of Figure 2–3, the greater $OB$ is relative to $OM$, the higher are the barriers to entry.) The greater the cost disadvantage of the small firm, the harder it is to start out at a scale that is inoffensively small and compete successfully. (In terms of the diagram, the more sharply the cost curve rises at outputs smaller than $OB$, the higher are the barriers to entry.)

Note that the incumbent and entrant are assumed to have the same costs, and thus the incumbent enjoys no *ex post* advantage if the entrant actually jumps into the market. The going firm benefits simply from being a "first-mover," having sunk the costs of its plant. Those sunk costs warn the potential entrant that the incumbent, if challenged, will fight rather than retreat from the market. The entrant therefore thinks twice before investing.

Several studies have attempted to measure economies of scale. The usual strategy is to measure the minimum efficient scale of output in the individual plant, then determine the number of such plants that we must stick together to make a firm that achieves any economies of multiplant operation. Table 2–2 summarizes the results of one careful study. It suggests that only moderate concentration is needed in most industries in order to enjoy the available economies of scale to the plant and the firm—at least for a nation as large as the United States. An earlier study by Bain also offered estimates of the disadvantage faced by plants and firms that are too small ($CD/OC$ in Figure 2–3); it was modest in most industries but formidable in a few.[4]

---

[4]Joe S. Bain, *Barriers to New Competition: Their Character and Consequences in Manufacturing Industries* (Cambridge, MA: Harvard University Press, 1956), Chap. 3.

**TABLE 2-2**  Estimates of Scale Economies in Plants and Multiplant Companies, Selected United States Manufacturing Industries, 1967

| Industry | Output of Efficient Plant as Percentage of National market (%) | Number of Efficient Plants Needed by Efficient Multiplant Firm | Share of U.S. Market Occupied by Efficient Firm, 1967 (%) |
|---|---|---|---|
| Beer brewing | 3.4 | 3–4 | 10–14 |
| Cigarettes | 6.6 | 1–2 | 6–12 |
| Broad-woven gray fabrics | 0.2 | 3–6 | 1 |
| Paints | 1.4 | 1 | 1.4 |
| Petroleum products | 1.9 | 2–3 | 4–6 |
| Shoes | 0.2 | 3–6 | 1 |
| Glass bottles | 1.5 | 3–4 | 4–6 |
| Cement | 1.7 | 1 | 2 |
| Steel mill products | 2.6 | 1 | 3 |
| Ball and roller bearings | 1.4 | 3–5 | 4.7 |
| Refrigerators | 14.1 | 4–8 | 14–20[a] |
| Automobile batteries | 1.9 | 1 | 2 |

[a]If refrigerators are manufactured along with other appliances; for an efficient firm specializing in refrigerators the national market share would be higher, as the first column shows.

*Source*: F. M. Scherer et al., *The Economics of Multi-Plant Operation: An International Comparisons Study* (Cambridge, MA: Harvard University Press, 1975), pp. 94, 336.

### Absolute-Cost Barriers to Entry

A second general type of impediment to entry goes by the name of *absolute-cost* barriers. It covers anything that makes the production cost curve of a new firm lie above that of a going concern. Figure 2–4 shows the new firm's cost curve placed above the old firm's by a constant amount. Note the distinction from scale-economy barriers to entry. Here the new firm faces a cost disadvantage over the old one *at any output level it chooses to produce*.

Absolute-cost barriers arise from many sources. Established firms may possess valuable know-how concerning production techniques. The going firm may have patents granting it exclusive rights to certain product features or processes, which the new firm can secure only by paying a royalty or spending the funds necessary to invent substitutes for them. Either way, its average costs lie above those of the going firm. Existing businesses that have made important discoveries may choose to patent them, in which case they are required by law to divulge their discoveries, or they may simply keep them a secret. A famous example is the secret ingredient that goes into Coca-Cola, a formula known only to a few executives of the firm. Again, and barring blind luck or espionage, the new firm has to spend money acquiring its own secret know-how.

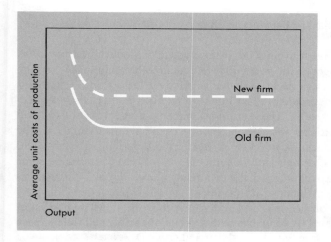

FIGURE 2-4 Barriers to entry due to absolute-cost disadvantages.

Another source of absolute-cost barriers to entry may be a limited supply of some especially significant input or factor of production. If the going firms have these cornered, they gain a cost advantage over entrants just as in the case of control over patents. Highly skilled and specialized personnel may all be attached to going firms. Industries based on minerals and metallic ores, such as copper refining, provide many examples. High-grade deposits often occur in only a small number of locations throughout the world. When they fall into the hands of existing processors or fabricators, the would-be entrant encounters a formidable absolute-cost barrier to entry in the expense of finding a new deposit. A new entrant to the industry, bidding for such scarce deposits, might drive up their price for the going firms as well as for itself. But the entrant cannot be sure this will happen, and at best faces a risk of disadvantage.

Some economists grumble about calling these first-mover advantages of the going firm barriers to entry. After all, the first seller had to find the bauxite deposit or invent the Coca-Cola formula. Why should we weep because the new entrant now faces the same start-up cost? The answer is that the going firms may monopolize or share in monopolizing the scarce and specialized input. The entrant finds itself paying a *higher* price for it than the going firms, not the same price as they paid.[5]

Still another absolute-cost barrier to entry can rest on the cost of capital to a new firm. Raising capital is itself a process subject to scale economies, because the lender incurs a similar cost to check out either a small or a large borrower. The lender may see lending to an entrant as riskier than lending to an incumbent simply because the incumbent has already established its organizational competence. The lender then charges the entrant more to borrow, elevating its costs above the incumbent's. Of course, a large firm already established in some other industry might not face this disadvantage.

[5]C. C. von Weizsäcker, *Barriers to Entry: A Theoretical Treatment* (New York: Springer Verlag, 1980), provided a subtle treatment of this and other normative issues relating to entry barriers.

### Product-Differentiation Barriers to Entry

A third source of barriers to entry lies in the element of product differentiation, discussed earlier. The successful going firm producing something like vacuum cleaners has a "name" established with the public. At least some households associate its name with desirable product traits—effective cleaning, long service-free life, ease of use, and so on. These attitudes make up a reservoir of good will for the firm, and its advertising and sales promotion need only maintain them. The new vacuum-cleaner producer, however, starts from scratch. Assuming that it solves the technical problems of design and manufacture, it still has to persuade some people to prefer its make over others that they already know. Figure 2–5 illustrates the disadvantage it faces. Suppose its machine has the same general physical characteristics as others on the market and that it spends the same proportion of sales revenue on advertising. It competes with a group of established sellers, each of whom we shall assume faces an identical demand curve D. All sellers operate on the same cost curve AC (which contains all of their costs except for advertising and sales promotion). The entrant will face a less favorable demand curve than the going firms, and its position will depend on the price they charge. If they choose the low price Pf, the entrant's potential demand is Df, so small that there is no scale at which the entrant can cover its costs. On the other hand, if the going firms charge as much as Pe, the entrant's expected demand curve shifts upward to De, and it just pays the entrant to produce quantity OE. Figure 2–5 illustrates both the effect of differentiation on the entrant's market opportunities and the

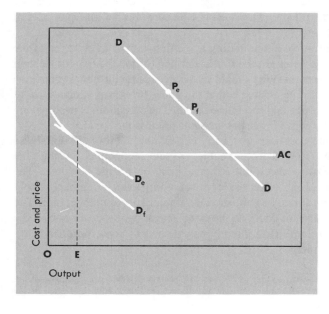

**FIGURE 2–5** Entry barriers due to product differentiation.

calculation that going firms can make of the highest price they can charge that just protects them from the threat of entry.[6]

Still, Figure 2–5 does not reveal exactly why the going firms enjoy demand curve $D$ and the entrant only $D_e$. Perhaps the established firms originally began no better known than the entrant, and had to invest just as heavily to make themselves known. In that case the entrant's cost of building goodwill cannot be presumed any greater than theirs. Even granting this possibility, there remain three reasons that entrants might be at a systematic disadvantage:

1. There may be scale economies in sales promotion, so that the large firm spending 10 percent of its sales revenues on advertising buys proportionally more messages than the small entrant spending the same percentage.
2. The effectiveness of the messages bought by the newcomer's advertising dollar may be less than that of the going firms' dollars, simply because they were there first. The newcomer seeking to establish its own goodwill must actually persuade people to forget the satisfaction they previously received from the going firms.
3. If there are scale economies in production, the absolute cost of the advertising outlay necessary to sell the output of an efficient plant may seriously inflate the entrant's total capital cost. An absolute capital-cost barrier to entry is either created or elevated.

In some industries these conditions can put entrants at a large disadvantage. Joe S. Bain estimated that an entrant would have to accept a price 10 to 25 percent lower than what going firms charge in such consumer-goods industries as gasoline, cigarettes, quality fountain pens, and automobiles.[7] No firms have entered the cigarette industry in recent decades despite all the changes in the product and increases in the number of brands offered by the going firms. We should stress, though, that product differentiation does not always create entry barriers. In some markets it eases the lot of the entrant who can pick a slightly different location, make a slightly different product, and run a viable business even at a small scale.

## Overall Importance of Entry Barriers

Unlike seller concentration, barriers to entry cannot be measured by looking up a few numbers in a government publication. For anything better than a broad impression, we have to make a close study industry by industry.

In some sectors of the American economy, a broad impression will suffice. The high turnover of firms in most service and retail-trade industries points directly to low entry barriers. The same holds for agriculture and forestry. Conversely, local public utilities and railroads reveal blockaded entry.

The manufacturing industries obviously present a mixed picture, and no such broad generalizations will do. We can turn back to Bain's early studies of over 30

[6]A sophisticated model of this asymmetry was provided by Richard Schmalensee, "Product Differentiation Advantages of Pioneering Brands," *American Economic Review*, Vol. LXXII (June 1982), pp. 349–365.

[7]Bain, *Barriers to New Competition*, pp. 127–129.

industries, mostly important ones, that sort them into categories that we can relate to Figure 2–2 (p. 23). The first group subject to high barriers to entry, which would allow the existing firms to set prices as much as 10 percent above minimum average costs without attracting more competitors, includes cigarettes, automobiles, quality fountain pens, nickel, and sulphur.[8] A class of moderate barriers, allowing prices 5 to 8 percent above average costs without entry, includes industries such as steel, copper, petroleum refining, biscuits, and soap. Meatpacking, rubber tires, cement, flour, and rayon fall among industries with low barriers to entry, permitting prices no more than 4 percent above average costs without attracting entry.[9] We also know, for this sample of manufacturing industries, which source of barriers is the culprit in the cases of moderate and high barriers. Scale economies in all cases would cause some perceptible entry barriers even if no other factors were present. But, contrary to what you might expect, scale economies explain few of the really high barriers. Here, product differentiation plays the leading role. Absolute-cost barriers, particularly in the form of heavy capital requirements, also explain some of the cases of moderate to high barriers.

## OTHER ELEMENTS OF MARKET STRUCTURE

Seller concentration, product differentiation, and barriers to entry do not conclude the list of important features in the environment of an industry. Remembering our goal of explaining the performance of American industries on the basis of their environmental or structural features, we could go on describing these features endlessly. We could summarize the legal framework within which an industry conducts its business. We could explore the industry's history to find out what "birth traumas" might have imprinted themselves on the present behavior patterns of firms. We could describe every aspect of the regional distribution of sellers and buyers. The list is interminable.

All this detail would not only clutter the picture but would also be scientifically unsound. The only features of structure worth examining are those that have some explanatory value. To possess this, they have to vary from one industry to another. Not only that, but they have to be associated with some observable variation in the behavior and performance of these industries. Thus, a lawyer might argue that laws that control the interpretation and enforcement of contracts improve the performance of American industries, for without them stable business relations would be impossible. True, but these laws affect all industries alike, and no one is talking of removing them. The point is valid, but not helpful for understanding differences among industries.

---

[8] Calling barriers to entry high because they permit a markup of price more than 10 percent above costs including normal profits does not prove that entry is actually or nearly blockaded. It could be that some of these industries would permit enormous rates of short-run profit if the present sellers had no concern about entry. The price elasticity of demand of course determines how high a monopolist would push the price in the absence of a threat of entry.

[9] Bain, *Barriers to New Competition*, pp. 169–172. Conditions in some of these industries have changed greatly since Bain's investigation, but comparable new estimates are not available.

## Buyer Concentration

The number of buyers in a market matters, logically speaking, just as much as the number of sellers. We fall into the habit of thinking of manufacturers who sell to many, many households. But in markets for producers' goods, the buyers— other manufacturing firms—often are not so numerous. Their bargaining power may then cut into the potential excess profits of an oligopolistic group of sellers. Studies have found that the more concentrated are its customers, the lower are the profits of a producer-good industry. The bargaining power of buyers also shows up in the finding that the smaller are the proportions of users' costs that their outputs account for, the more profitable are producer-good industries. The value of being an unimportant supplier presumably arises because buyers focus their bargaining wiles on important inputs.[10] Buyer concentration can affect consumer-good industries too. The maker of quality watches sells not directly to the public but to jewelry stores and similar outlets. To reach prospective final buyers in a city, the manufacturing firm must persuade these outlets to handle its watches—and the suitable outlets may be few in number and drive a hard bargain! John Kenneth Galbraith advanced the doctrine of "countervailing power" to suggest that, where sellers of manufactures are concentrated, the retailer buyers will coalesce and become concentrated in order to strike a better bargain. This form of tit-for-tat may occur sometimes, but it hardly counts as a sure thing.

The retail sector may wield bargaining power over the manufacturer in yet another way. For some kinds of goods—automobiles, clothing, stereo equipment— the final buyer depends on the retail outlet for advice, information, service, or even just a general ambience that aids the buyer in making a choice. Many of the retail outlets that sell these products thus play an important role in forming or developing the customer's attitude toward the competing brands that are available. The retailer thus puts the finishing touches on the product differentiation sought by the manufacturer, and the manufacturer must offer a deal sweet enough to induce the retailer to perform this job. Conversely, other consumer goods are sold through "convenience outlets" such as supermarkets, in which the householder neither expects nor requests advice from the store's personnel. The buyer's choice among brands depends heavily on the manufacturer's advertising, and when the manufacturer has successfully promoted a product to the public through advertising, the retailer cannot credibly threaten not to stock it. The retailer loses bargaining power against the manufacturer. In this analysis, the retailer's bargaining power (or lack of it) depends on the nature of product differentiation. This consideration is quite independent of the effect of many or few competing retailers on the bargaining process.[11]

[10]S. R. Lustgarten, "The Impact of Buyer Concentration in Manufacturing Industries," *Review of Economics and Statistics*, Vol. LVII (August 1975), pp. 125–132; Ralph M. Bradburd, "Price-Cost Margins in Producer Goods Industries and "The Importance of Being Unimportant'," *Review of Economics and Statistics*, Vol. LXIV (August 1982), pp. 405–412.

[11]Michael E. Porter, *Interbrand Choice, Strategy, and Bilateral Market Power* (Cambridge, MA: Harvard University Press, 1976).

### Sunk Costs and Barriers to Exit

The production of some goods requires heavy investment by the firm in fixed plant and equipment, and the outlay involved is subject to risk. If the business fails, the plant may have little salvage value. If the demand for coal should die away, the mine owner will find few buyers for a hole in the ground. If the market should merely turn sick, our seller and any competitors would keep up their production levels, because the fixed costs cannot be avoided by cutting back output. Their sustained output, in face of a reduced demand, means much lower prices and profits. Fixed costs are thus likely to influence the character of competition and to goad sellers to search for ways to reduce their risks. One possible method is to enter into collusive agreements to keep up the price.[12]

Sunk costs are an important element of market structure because they impede the exit of resources from a market. Put another way, the seller who must invest in durable and specific production assets in order to operate in a market thereby becomes subject to barriers to exit should things go badly. The resource commitments that represent exit barriers are in fact closely connected to the sources of entry barriers, described earlier. Indeed, in order to repel a determined entrant, an incumbent *must* have some fixed commitments to a market: "Here I am, and here I stay." There cannot be entry barriers without exit barriers.

### Demand Growth

Consider two industries, one facing a total demand unchanged from year to year, the other with a total demand growing rapidly. What differences can we expect in their behavior? Economists have offered several answers to this question, and the answers point in different directions for their effect on competition. The following hypotheses illustrate the possibilities:

1. Market demand grows fast enough that firms have their hands full just expanding their production capacities. Even if new entrants are coming in, there is little incentive to fight for market share. Producers are likely to honor oligopolistic agreements with each other, and profits are apt to be high.
2. Assume that the product is differentiated, and that having a large market share this year makes it easier for a firm to claim a large market share next year. (Last year's automobile is a rolling advertisement for this year's.) The faster the market is growing, the more it pays the firm to fight to enlarge its current market share. That is because the enlarged present share promises an enlarged future share, and with it a greater present value of the profits the firm can expect to earn in the future. But fast growth implies more competition and lower profits in the short run.

[12]One can distinguish between costs that are *sunk* (cannot be avoided even if the firm quits producing) and costs that are *fixed* (do not vary with its level of output). The "contestable markets" school of economists urged this distinction and proposed that some monopolists might incur fixed costs that are not sunk. Such an incumbent could not earn any excess profits without being undercut by an entrant. No significant live examples have been found of costs that are fixed but not sunk, so we ignore the distinction.

These two scenarios imply different relationships between growth and profits; the first says that high growth brings high profits, and the second says that growth brings low profits when it first speeds up. The statistical evidence generally supports the former result, but we might expect to observe different patterns in different industries.

### Import Competition

We noted in Chapter 1 that the process of defining the market sometimes compels compromises that leave significant sellers on the outside. Competition from imports provides the most prominent example for many U.S. manufacturing industries. Anyone would nowadays include numerous foreign firms among the group of sellers of automobiles in the United States. In other industries, such as steel, imports represent a significant but less important or more sporadic force. Foreign sellers can be disadvantaged in the market for many reasons. Their transportation costs may be high; American tastes may favor U.S.-produced varieties of a differentiated product; or American producers may simply be efficient and have lower costs of production.

We habitually measure import competition by the share of sales in a market accounted for by foreign producers. When these shares are large or are increasing rapidly, import competition lands in the realm of politics as domestic producers seek the government's help in stifling the competition. As the theory of entry barriers shows, what really matters is the degree to which imports would overrun the market if domestic producers raised their prices much above competitive levels.

## MARKET STRUCTURE OVER TIME

Knowing the potential effects of market structure can prove helpful for public policy only if an industry's market structure is stable. If an industry's entry barriers are high today and low tomorrow, we have little hope of understanding or influencing them. We must now ask whether the main elements of market structure are stable, and whether we can explain changes when they do occur.

### Stability of Market Structure

The average level of seller concentration in United States manufacturing industries has changed little over the last 80 years. Is that because concentration in each industry has tended to stay constant, or because the industries themselves have changed in offsetting ways? The former answer seems more nearly correct. If we take a group of comparable industries and rank them by seller concentration, both in 1900 and today, we will find the ranks similar.[13]

---

[13]For evidence, see Saul S. Sands, "Concentration in U.S. Manufacturing Industry, 1904–1947," *International Economic Review*, Vol. III (January 1962), pp. 79–93.

The same stability holds for the major elements of market structure. The level of product differentiation seems to change slowly in most industries. Although such changes can be significant over a long period of years, it is hard to think of many industries where they have occurred. Grandma bought her crackers from a cracker barrel, whereas crackers now come in brightly differentiated packages. Indeed, the amount of differentiation may have swung upward in many industries during the past century. But nowadays we seldom see an industry change quickly from selling an undifferentiated to a differentiated product. We lack any direct data on changes in barriers to entry over time, but they give the same general impression of stability. Entry restrictions rest largely on product differentiation, scale economies, and other such elements, which seem to change slowly.

## Explaining Changes in Market Structure

Where market structure *does* change substantially, the process can often be easily explained. This is because the different elements of market structure influence one another. Some combinations can occur together quite logically. But other combinations, like green socks and a blue suit, just do not match. High barriers to entry and low concentration would come as a surprise. High barriers tend to shut off the flow of new firms into an industry. Because a firm disappears from time to time, due to natural causes, the number of sellers remaining is sure to fall. If the barriers remain high, concentration is likely to rise.

Because the elements of an industry's market structure are linked, changes in one structural element often explain why another one is changing. An example sheds light on the process. For instance, just after World War I, a major increase seems to have occurred in the level of product differentiation in the young automobile industry. Being an inherently complex gadget, the auto had been differentiated from the early days of Henry Ford. But the level and character of differentiation changed greatly at that time and, with it, the barriers to entry and concentration in the industry.

> During the period prior to the early 1920s, the automobile rose to prominence in the American economy. The development of a mass market was achieved through the exploitation of tremendous economies of scale, associated with the assembly-line method of production developed originally by Henry Ford. Ford concentrated his energies on mass-producing at low costs, dropping the price of the Model T from $950 in 1909 to $290 in 1925. It was at this time that Ford used to make his famous announcement that "any customer can have a car painted any color that he wants so long as it is black."
>
> In the decade after World War I, the nature of automobile demand changed radically. The automobile market shifted toward being a saturated or replacement market. This opened the door to sales based on factors other than dependable transportation at low cost, and the handle was grasped eagerly by General Motors. A highly differentiated Chevrolet was introduced, which sold for about $100 more than the Model T but which offered more attractive styling, greater speed, and a number of other features. Ford's market share fell drastically, from 55 percent in 1921 to slightly more than one-third in 1926.

The increased product differentiation resulting from this change altered a number of other structural features in the industry. Substantial barriers to entry were raised, which were due to the consumer loyalty engendered by individual products, to the higher resale values of established cars, and to large advertising expenditures.

It was thus made clear to potential entrants that greater efforts and higher costs were required to obtain a niche in the market. Even if a new entrant could achieve equal or superior productive efficiency, effective entry would not be possible unless the obstacle of demand creation was overcome. During the early years of industrial growth, entry had been relatively easy. In the 15 years between 1906 and 1920, a total of 126 firms had entered the automobile industry, and the turnover of firms was quite high. In later years the total number of new entrants declined sharply, and no permanently successful entry has occurred since the formation of the Chrysler Corporation in the early 1920s.

By blockading entry, the rise in effective product differentiation has greatly increased the level of concentration. There were 84 firms in the industry in 1920, but this figure had dropped to 44 by 1926. In the 5 years between 1922 and 1926, a total of 52 firms left the industry. With the end of the period of rapid growth in demand, widespread product differentiation created severe disadvantages for firms without established reputations. The decline has continued until the present. Now only three domestic mass-producers of automobiles remain, although foreign companies have grown much more prominent.

Industries also sometimes show sudden declines in the level of concentration. These can just as well reflect changes in other elements of market structure. Take one segment of the chemicals industry, the segment producing synthetic ammonia. Before World War II, two firms accounted for almost 90 percent of United States production. Apparently this very high level of concentration reflected economies of scale at the plant level, so that a very few plants could supply the whole prewar demand. World War II produced a great expansion of demand for synthetic ammonia, which served both as an ingredient in high explosives and as a component of fertilizer for a rapidly expanding U.S. agriculture. At this point the government stepped in and built a number of synthetic ammonia plants itself, owning at the end of the war more than did the private producers. When the United States sold off its wartime industrial plants to private industry, it chose to sell its synthetic ammonia capacity to firms new to the industry, raising the number of sellers to 12. When the Korean War came, almost the same series of developments occurred. Instead of building up ammonia capacity itself, the government chose to encourage private firms to expand output. But those encouraged were largely new to the industry, and again the effect was to raise the number of producing firms from 12 to 24.

These changes in concentration, brought on by a rapid growth of demand supported by government policy, had a lasting effect on seller concentration. By 1957 the largest four firms accounted for only 39 percent of ammonia capacity. The one-time power of scale-economy barriers to entry to hold up the concentration level had been broken.[14]

[14]W. H. Martin, "Public Policy and Increased Competition in the Synthetic Ammonia Industry," *Quarterly Journal of Economics*, Vol. LXXIII (August 1959), pp. 373–392.

In short, a logic controls the relations among the elements of market structure. High concentration is not likely to persist for long periods of time after high barriers to entry are pulled down. On the other hand, the rise of substantial product differentiation can erect barriers to entry and thereby increase the level of concentration. Like oranges in the bottom of a round bowl, few major elements of market structure will stay put when one of them is moved.

## SUMMARY

Price theory tells us that highly concentrated sellers may earn excess profits and misallocate the nation's limited stock of factors of production. Concentration, however, is not the only feature of an industry that can be significant for economic welfare. The economic environment surrounding the firms in an industry contains other important elements as well, and these, together with seller concentration, are known as the market structure.

*Product differentiation* is one of these major features of market structure. It exists when consumers form different preferences among the individual brands of a product. It removes the pressure on producers all to sell at a single market price. Each firm can set its own price policy, and the form of price competition is changed.

*Barriers to entry* comprise another vital feature of market structure. They affect the supply of potential rivals to firms in an industry. They arise from scale economies, "absolute cost" elements, and product differentiation. The latter two put the costs of a new firm above those of an established one. We can measure entry barriers by determining how high the market price can be raised without attracting entry. Entry barriers depend on some type of first-mover advantage for the incumbent firm. In the case of scale economies, the advantage lies *only* in the incumbent's prior commitment to the market of capacity that the entrant cannot profitably displace.

We can identify many other elements of market structure, although seller concentration, product differentiation, and entry barriers seem to make the most difference in practice. Other candidates would include buyer concentration, fixed costs, the rate of growth of demand, and import competition.

All these elements of market structure tend to be stable over time. No industry has high barriers to entry this year, low barriers next year. The elements of market structure, however, are all interrelated. Any change in one tends to bring about changes in another. By noting this relation, we can often explain why seller concentration has changed.

---

# Chapter 3

# The Large Corporation

---

General Motors employs more people than live in the city of Boston. Exxon Corporation's sales are larger than the gross national products of more than 100 countries. In 1982 the largest 100 manufacturing corporations accounted for one-third of all value added by manufacture in the United States.

Large corporations are such a conspicuous part of our economy and society that their importance seems self-evident. Some people charge that they create compelling political and social problems—that they bribe elected officials, pollute the environment, or provide deplorable working conditions on their assembly lines. Although we cannot investigate them here, these charges are important.

Our concern is with the big company in the market for its product. Its significance there is far from obvious. Economic theory has much to say about companies that are big *relative to their markets*, as we saw in Chapters 1 and 2. But what does it matter that a company is large *absolutely*? Most large companies hold big shares of sales in their principal markets. But consequences that develop from absolute size—beyond the giant firm's dominance of its chief market—probably arise because the firm spills beyond that market into many others. That spillover can take three forms. The giant can be

1. *Diversified* into other product markets.
2. *Vertically integrated*, to supply its own raw materials, or distribute its own products.
3. *Multinational*, to carry out similar activities in other countries.

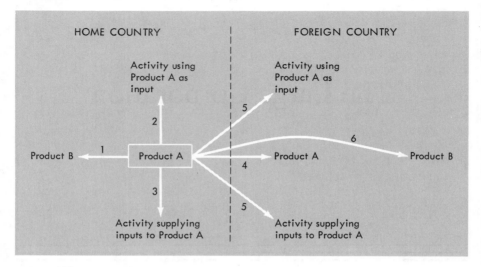

1 - Diversified company
2 - Company vertically integrated forward
3 - Company vertically integrated backward
4 - Multinational company making horizontal foreign investment
5 - Multinational company making vertical foreign investment
6 - Multinational company making diversified foreign investment

**FIGURE 3–1**    Types of companies with multimarket operations.

Figure 3–1 provides a visual comparison of these three corporate forms, in terms of the ways in which a company making product *A* can extend its activities into other markets. A diversified company is sometimes called a "conglomerate," but we shall avoid that term; it implies that there is no relation between products *A* and *B*, whereas we shall see that a diversified company's activities are often economically related. Multinational companies often produce the same goods abroad as they do at home, in which case we call them horizontal foreign investments. (They resemble some domestic firms, such as large bakeries, that extend their activities from one regional market to another.) Multinational companies also undertake vertical integration across national boundaries—especially in the form of backward integration—and sometimes make diversified foreign investments.

## LARGE COMPANIES IN THE U.S. ECONOMY

Large corporations apparently accounted for a growing proportion of activity in the U.S. economy from 1929 to around 1960—a trend much remarked upon and much lamented. But then the trend apparently petered out, despite conspicuous waves of mergers among big companies in the late 1960s, late 1970s, and the 1980s. Even the recent large wave of mergers has apparently not changed this situation: The largest companies do less than their *proportional* share of merging. In the manufacturing sector the largest 100 companies' share of value added rose from 23 percent in 1947 to 33 percent in 1963, but was still stalled at that figure in 1982. For the nonfinancial sector as a whole the data are rougher but appear to tell the same story, with the share of the largest 100 steady at just under one-third of total nonfinancial assets.[1]

Still, these shares held by the largest companies strike many people as high. What we make of their dominance depends partly on how much turnover takes place in the ranks of the leaders. The largest companies today were not the largest 50 years ago, and the frequency with which their leadership turns over surely indicates whether their dominant positions are fixed or transient. Of the top 50 manufacturing companies in 1955, 27 remained in the top 50 for 1990. Of the 23 newcomers in 1990, only five were not in the top 500 in 1955.

There is some turnover in industrial leadership. Our best evidence suggests that the turnover of firms in the top ranks has probably dropped in the last 60 years. Some viewers have feared that a reduced turnover rate portends some hardening of the industrial arteries and decreased competitiveness of our economy. Another explanation is the increasing importance of diversification—operating in many different product markets. Companies used to ride into or out of industrial leadership when their principal industries grew or shrank as proportions of total economic activity. But the process of diversification increasingly allows a large firm stuck in a slow-growing sector to hoist anchor and sustain its growth rate by expanding into other industries. When the cigarette companies grew fearful in the 1960s that health hazards associated with smoking would curb the growth of their market, they diversified into chewing gum, snack foods, wine, distilled liquor, pet food—becoming, as someone put it, an "oral gratification industry."

## DIVERSIFICATION

Why do companies diversify? We can better assess what diversification does to the economy once we know why it occurs. The example of the cigarette companies is instructive. The possibility that demand for cigarettes might decline, or that the government would act to restrict cigarette consumption, placed the companies in a risky situation. These threats to prospects for profit in cigarettes would not affect the market for cat food, and they might even boost the demand for liquor (if people embraced a new vice when they forswore the old one). The diversified company would face less risk to its profitability and survival. Even if profit rates in its new businesses were no higher than they had been in cigarettes, it could come out earning the same overall profit rate with less uncertainty.

Another cause of diversification revealed by the cigarette companies' experience is the opportunity for diversifying firms to use their established capabilities in new lines of business. The tobacco firms had learned a great deal about how to develop and promote products in ways that would attract buyers, and they had

[1]See Lawrence J. White, "What Has Been Happening to Aggregate Concentration in the United States?" *Journal of Industrial Economics*, Vol. XXIX (March 1981), pp. 223–230.

substantial knowledge of distribution channels for nondurable consumer goods. These intangible assets might find profitable uses in other businesses such as snack foods. The company that successfully applies its established capabilities to a new line of business can make more productive use of a fixed asset—that intangible capability—and thereby raise the economy's productivity. We know, for example, that companies' research activities frequently bring into their hands knowledge and innovations that are valuable in other industries, so a lot of diversification takes place both into and out of highly innovative industries as firms seek to make full use of their technological assets.

Another virtue of diversification is that it may amount to entry into an industry and thus effectively reduce the force of barriers to entry (described in Chapter 2). If an established company enters a market by building a new plant, or if it acquires a going firm and improves its effectiveness, the level of competition in the market is probably raised. Some going firms are likely to have advantages against a given industry's barriers to entry. Their liquid funds and good credit ratings can boost them over entry barriers due to absolute capital cost. And their established trademarks and marketing skills can sometimes be effective against product-differenti-ation entry barriers. Going-firm entrants still cede some advantage to firms already entrenched in any market guarded by entry barriers, but the market power that those barriers can sustain is generally less when going firms can enter than if they were denied the right to diversify. This fact builds a case for the diversified company. Several studies suggest that the prototype industry favored for diversified expansion is one with good growth prospects, especially from high technology, and surrounded by moderate entry barriers. Mountainous entry barriers stop even the large established firm; low barriers warn the company that the industry holds no prospect for better-than-normal profits.

Some causes of diversification, however, have less favorable implications for economic efficiency. During the late 1960s diversification became a fad for many companies, and they diversified for the sake of rapid growth and without much heed to profit or efficiency. Tax gimmicks were blamed for many conglomerate mergers, along with the gullibility of a public that would—temporarily, at least—pay prices for the shares of "swinging conglomerates" that in the end were unjustified by their profit performance.[2] The merger wave of the 1980s looks only slightly more rational. About half the time the stock-market value of a firm's shares falls when it makes a big acquisition, which means that the share-owning public thinks the transaction lowers their company's probable future earnings. Worse yet, large companies' many *ex post* failures to integrate and use their acquisitions effectively make one wonder whether the shareholders have been pessimistic enough.[3]

[2]The evidence was summarized by Peter O. Steiner, *Mergers: Motives, Effects, Policies* (Ann Arbor: University of Michigan Press, 1975).

[3]Several studies have found that managers who are relatively free of control by their shareholders (see Chapter 1) are more likely to undertake mergers that reduce their shareholders' wealth. See Victor L. You et al., "Mergers and Bidders' Wealth: Managerial and Strategic Factors," *The Economics of Strategic Planning*, L. G. Thomas, III, ed. (Lexington, MA: Lexington Books, 1986), pp. 201–221.

### Diversification and the Market's Structure

The significance of diversification for a market's operation emerges when we interpret it as an element of market structure. How can the diversification of a market's participants affect competitive processes in the market and thereby its social performance? As we answer this question, diversification reveals some disadvantages for society.

First, the large, diversified tenant of a market can potentially use the profits it earns elsewhere to discipline or even destroy its rivals in the market at hand. For example, it can lower its price, financing its own losses out of profits from other markets, and force losses on a rival until he quits. Driving out a rival can be profitable in some cases—if the cost to the predator is not too great, and if entry is slow or difficult enough so that supernormal profits can be enjoyed after the rival's demise. There is a great popular fear that large companies will use the "long purse" to drive out rivals who are smaller or less favorably situated, although overtly aggressive actions are thoroughly illegal under United States laws. Whether because of the laws, or because predatory actions are in fact seldom profitable, the number of clear-cut cases of documented predation is small. Although few large firms in recent decades have been caught with the smoking gun, the possibility remains that their potential strength in a competitive struggle tames their single-market rivals, causes potential entrants to think twice, and thereby impairs the effectiveness of competition.

A lesser but still tangible danger is that diversified companies can conceal their profits from any one market in a consolidated income statement that covers all their activities. The potential entrant sizing up an industry populated by diversified companies has trouble telling whether prospective profits are merely normal or beyond the dreams of avarice. The disciplining force of entry is blunted when the potential entrant becomes less certain of his prospects. Entry barriers are effectively raised. But there is also a disadvantage to society if a diversified company conceals not profits but losses in a particular business. A firm's managers can hide their mistakes from the stockholders long after bad investments should have been admitted and terminated.

## VERTICAL INTEGRATION

A company can also spill beyond the boundaries of any one market by being vertically integrated. We say it is integrated backward from market $A$ if it produces inputs into product $A$ as well as $A$ itself. And the company that is integrated forward produces $A$ and undertakes further processing of $A$ or operates distributive outlets to put $A$ into the hands of final buyers. Like diversification, vertical integration can affect a firm's behavior in any of its markets. To understand those effects, we first inquire why vertical integration comes about.

By integrating, a company can sometimes attain real economies in production. Steel ingots can be converted into structural shapes more cheaply if they are worked before cooling so as to avoid the cost of reheating them. To accomplish this, the processes of ingot production and fabrication must be physically adjacent and closely coordinated—difficult between independent companies. Another economy of vertical integration lies in cutting the costs of arm's-length transactions. An advantage of chain grocery stores lies in central buying of the many things they sell, which avoids the need for a different salesperson to call on each store to peddle each brand of corn flakes or margarine.

Vertical integration can also come as a response to the elements of market structure surrounding a firm. Consider the market for iron ore. Large deposits of iron ore are not very numerous, nor are large steel companies. The producer of iron ore must make an enormous fixed investment, its profitability dependent on the terms it can get for ore sold to the steel companies. The steelmakers' own heavy investments likewise depend on access to supplies of ore. Uncertainty hangs heavily over such a market with few buyers and sellers, each one lodged in a risky situation. Vertical integration between buyers and sellers relieves both of the uncertainty about the bargain they could strike in the open market.

Vertical integration also responds to market structure when companies integrate forward to gain the advantages of product differentiation. Consider a group of oligopolists producing a relentlessly undifferentiable product, such as copper. Without product differentiation to insulate their market shares, they may find it difficult to achieve and sustain a stable consensus. But when they integrate forward to produce pots and pans and other copper articles that carry brand names, they can achieve some differentiation and stabilize the consensus. Likewise, many manufacturers bolster their market power by controlling the distributive outlets for their product—if not by vertical integration, then by franchises and long-term exclusive contracts with independent retailers. The retail outlets of the gasoline refiners are an important example, as were those of the domestic automobile producers when they handled a single maker's vehicles exclusively.

### Effects of Vertical Integration

Markets are affected by the presence of companies that have grown large through vertical integration. The competitive position of nonintegrated sellers can suffer. Major aluminum producers are integrated forward into the production of fabricated aluminum articles. Nonintegrated competitors also operate in the aluminum fabrication business. The integrated producers can potentially put the "squeeze" on these independents by raising the price of aluminum ingots while holding constant the price of fabricated aluminum. The nonintegrated producers' price-cost margins shrink while those of the integrated producers stay unchanged; a squeeze can induce the nonintegrated producers to go along with collusive strategies or even to depart from the market. Admittedly, if the integrated producers jointly monopolize aluminum ingots there may be no further gain from monopolizing aluminum fabrication as well. That is, under special assumptions there exists one maximum lump of monopoly profit potentially to be earned in the whole economic chain of processes that starts with aluminum ore and ends with finished articles delivered into the final user's hands. If you capture that lump at one processing stage, there is no more monopoly profit to accrue at another stage, and thus no reason to squeeze out competitors. The proposition need not apply, however, when each stage is oligopolistic. Then the vertically integrated producers probably capture less than that maximum lump of monopoly profit, and they may gain more of it by weakening or destroying their rivals in any one of the vertically related markets.

Just as vertical integration can impair competition when it facilitates a squeeze on unintegrated rivals, it also threatens potential entrants and effectively raises the barriers to entry. A dilemma faces the potential entrant to any market stage in which most of the going firms are vertically integrated. Suppose that the newcomer enters into aluminum fabrication when 90 percent of the production of both aluminum ingots and fabricated aluminum is controlled by vertically integrated firms. If it buys from an integrated ingot producer, it faces the risk of a price squeeze. If it buys from an ingot producer who is not vertically integrated, it can draw on only 10 percent of the industry's ingot capacity and might find itself dealing in a thin market. Either way, there is a risk. The entrant avoids this problem, of course, if it enters as an integrated producer. But that strategy may be brought up short by capital-cost barriers to entry if one of the stages is large-scale and capital-intensive. The entrant who takes the plunge can choose between the costs of integrated entry and the risks of unintegrated entry so as to minimize the disadvantage. But the point is that some net disadvantage plagues the entrant, whichever choice is made.

> The aluminum industry illustrates the various aspects of vertical integration. Before World War II, the Aluminum Company of America (Alcoa) possessed a monopoly of production in the United States. The firm was integrated backward into supplying itself with ore and generating the considerable amount of electricity needed to produce aluminum. This integration was suspected to increase the barriers to entry, and indeed Alcoa's monopoly was ended only by public-policy decisions on the disposal of production capacity built by the U.S. government during World War II. Today's international aluminum industry includes a moderate number of suppliers, with the large ones still integrated vertically. Integration backward into ore and the initial refining stage occurs because these activities are large-scale and must be conducted next to one another in remote geographic locations. Without integration the parties would commit heavy investments in a bilateral monopoly situation, at risk in whatever haggling and bargaining might then occur. The U.S. primary aluminum producers are integrated forward to varying extents into making various fabricated aluminum products. Analysis of differences among products in degree of integration has confirmed the role of the quest for product differentiation and other strategies for benefitting from differences in fabricated products' demand elasticities. Also, forward integration serves the interest of efficient short-run adjustment that arises because aluminum ingot prices in the short run do not always move to clear the market, so that some customers at times may get rationed out.[4]

[4]John A. Stuckey, *Vertical Integration and Joint Ventures in the Aluminum Industry* (Cambridge, MA: Harvard University Press, 1983).

## THE MULTINATIONAL COMPANY

The multinational company deals in more than one national market. Although multinationals are no new invention, they have become much more numerous since World War II. And they have become highly controversial—first outside the United States, but more recently at home as well. Of the 500 largest manufacturing companies listed by *Fortune* magazine, one-third (187) had carried on operations in six or more foreign countries by 1967. By 1982 U.S.-based multinationals were making sales through their foreign affiliates that were 42 percent as large as their sales in the United States. The extent of foreign operations varied greatly among industries. Makers of medical instruments sold 60 percent as much abroad as at home, pharmaceutical manufacturers 42 percent, and ferrous metal companies only 10 percent.

Operating in other countries is obviously a way for a company to grow beyond the scope of its principal product market in the United States. For that reason, multinational status should be considered beside diversification and vertical integration. But there are deeper reasons for grouping these characteristics of the large firm. The company that invests abroad is, in a sense, diversifying. Many multinational firms make and sell lines of products abroad that are quite similar to those they make and sell at home. But they are still diversifying geographically and can enjoy gains from spreading risks across countries similar to those of the company diversifying across product lines. Other multinationals invest abroad to produce raw materials or manufactured components that are inputs to their principal products in the United States. That form of foreign investment is simply vertical integration that happens to spill across a national boundary. We shall call it vertical foreign investment and denote as horizontal the foreign investments of companies that make the same lines of goods abroad as at home. (Some foreign investments are diversifications across product as well as geographic boundaries; these are minor though increasing.)

### Causes of Foreign Investment

The reasons for vertical foreign investment are basically the same as for any form of vertical integration. Many large-scale foreign investments are undertaken to secure raw materials that require large-scale capital-intensive methods of production. Sometimes the parent company wants the raw materials to feed its manufacturing processes at home. Sometimes it merely deals in these raw materials, selling them on the world market to make profitable use of the knowledge it has acquired of the relevant markets.

Horizontal direct investment, however, is trickier to explain. If there are any economies of scale in making vacuum cleaners, why does not the multinational home-appliance company simply produce them all in the cheapest location and export to other markets around the world? One answer is that there may be no one "cheapest location"; because of transportation costs and tariffs the company may serve some or most of its national markets economically from local production facilities. Another answer is the presence of our old friend, the structural trait of product differentiation. The company that has differentiated its product successfully in its home market gains a brand name and some intangible skills at designing and presenting its product so that it attracts buyers. These intangible skills and assets, once won in a single national market, are available for use in other national markets as well. To support these marketing abilities the company needs production facilities abroad that can adapt to local conditions and (perhaps) reassure buyers about the company's continuing commitment to the market. We are not surprised to find that horizontal foreign investment is most common in highly differentiated products—food processing, pharmaceuticals, consumer durables, computers, and the like. Makers of undifferentiated goods less commonly become multinational even when they are big companies with dominant shares in their home markets.

> These forces explaining the development of horizontal foreign investment are illustrated by the food processing industry. Many of the leading firms in the U.S. industry first rose to national prominence by successfully developing a single product. Others succeeded by developing efficient distribution networks that could handle numbers of otherwise unrelated food products destined for the same grocery stores. The former group of firms that succeeded through heavy advertising (product differentiation) are the ones that have become heavily multinational. As food markets in foreign countries have grown more similar to the U.S. model, these companies could repeat their earlier success stories in foreign markets, especially with convenience foods and other items amenable to heavy sales promotion. The American food processers have been especially attracted to large national markets abroad, countries well saturated with television, and already well exposed to things American—all ingredients of success for the firm specializing in product differentiation.[5]

## Multinationality and Market Behavior

The big multinational company's participation in a market has many of the same consequences we assigned to diversified or vertically integrated companies. It is valuable as an actual—and potential—entrant into national markets. Several foreign auto makers have begun producing vehicles within the United States; it is doubtful that any company not a producer of automobiles abroad could consider undertaking large-scale production in America. In many industries abroad, it appears that the multinationals increase the amount of rivalry and bring many products into the market. As we suggested previously, many U.S. industries have grown more competitive as the domestic market has been invaded by strong companies based overseas that use some combination of investment in American factories and export shipments from home base.

However, multinationals may have adverse effects on competition once their industries settle into mature international oligopolies. Like the diversified company, the multinational has a long purse. It can potentially use its strength in a competitive struggle to discipline or expel weaker rivals dependent on the national market. With

---

[5]Thomas Horst, *At Home Abroad: A Study of the Domestic and Foreign Operations of the American Food-Processing Industry* (Cambridge, MA: Ballinger, 1974).

multinationals spreading across the major national markets, we wonder about their effect on the *international* market. That is, what happens when the same oligopolists come to face each other in one national market after another? The motive to live and let live may be strengthened. Multinational company *A* considers trying to capture share from *B* in the French market. But *A* pauses to reflect that its German subsidiary is in a relatively weak position and ripe for retaliation by *B*'s German subsidiary. Mutual forebearance may be the best course. The international farm tractor industry may illustrate such transnational oligopoly behavior, because it is otherwise hard to understand how North American prices could for years have been held well above their level in the United Kingdom—a low-cost producer—without somebody loading a westbound boat full of British-made tractors.[6]

## BIGNESS AND MARKET STRUCTURE

Our strategy for examining the large company has been to separate the effects of its size (and share) in a particular market from other sources of large absolute size. In the process, "bigness" itself has emerged as an element of the structures of markets. A market of given concentration, entry barriers, product differentiation, and so on may behave differently when the firms operating in it expand their extramarket activities. And the change will depend on whether the extramarket expansion takes the form of product-market diversification, vertical integration, or foreign investment.

The surprising fact may not be that corporate bigness emerges as an element of market structure, but rather that it fails to dominate all the rest. Our society tends to believe in the intrinsic virtue of the little fellow, but at the same time it assumes that bigger is better and stronger. How, then, can small firms survive in the shadow of corporate giants? In the same spirit, many foreigners who see the markets of their nations populated by subsidiaries of large multinational companies ask how their own national firms can survive the threat of the international giants.

The evidence that we examined in the first two chapters of this book supplies part of the answer. While the dominance of large corporations in the American economy has increased overall, seller concentration in the average industrial market has risen little if any. (Concentration has risen lately in some other industrial countries, but that is because they permit mergers between large competing firms and apply government policies to encourage concentration in some sectors.) Furthermore, we observe many industries in which large and small firms have long coexisted. Bigness sometimes brings advantages (and higher profits), but that does not mean the big fish always eat the small fish. Scale economies place small firms at a disadvantage, but the disadvantage is not significant in every industry. Product differentiation builds entry barriers and promotes concentration in some markets, but it also protects the small firm that has found a profitable niche in the market.

[6]Robert T. Kudrle, *Agricultural Tractors: A World Industry Study* (Cambridge, MA: Ballinger, 1975). Chap. 10.

We saw in this chapter that big firms can threaten small firms by dipping into the deep pocket, but big firms also threaten other big firms because they have advantages for scaling certain barriers to entry. There is no convincing evidence that the presence of large firms in a market tends to make it more concentrated, although if a market becomes more concentrated its typical firm must necessarily be getting bigger.

If corporate size does not dominate the elements of market structure, it does join them. We have suggested various specific ways in which the assets and activities of a large firm outside any one of its markets can influence its behavior within that market. But a more general point lies behind those examples, and it turns on the concept of "corporate strategy" used in the study of business administration. A company's strategy is its long-run plan for making the most of its organizational strengths and minimizing its weaknesses in order to assure its profitability and survival.[7] A central feature of a large company's strategy is the extent of its multimarket activity (in all forms described in this chapter) and the relations among its various businesses. Two large multimarket firms competing in the same industry often follow quite different strategies, reflected in differing relations of the business at hand to the rest of the companies' operations. For one firm this market may serve to dispose of a by-product from some other process; for a second, it may be the end of a chain of vertically related production processes. That is, the strategic relation between the business at hand and the rest of the company may differ greatly for the two participants in the market.

These strategic differences carry an important implication for market conduct. As we shall see in Chapter 4, monopoly profits can be reaped in a market populated by a small group of sellers only if they can agree to some extent not to compete with one another. To reach such an agreement and make it stick, they must coordinate many aspects of their market conduct as well as their responses to any unexpected disturbances that come along. The more diverse are their strategies, the harder this coordination becomes, and the less likely are joint monopoly profits to be captured.

## SUMMARY

Large firms often hold large shares in their principal markets. But to understand the corporate giant's economic importance apart from its market dominance, we must analyze the activities it may undertake outside its base market: diversification, vertical integration, and foreign investment. This analysis is important because large corporations prevail in many industrial sectors, and their prevalence was increasing at least up to the 1960s.

Diversification spreads risks, allows fuller utilization of the firm's capabilities, and comprises entry by established firms into markets that might otherwise have been insulated by entry barriers. But diversification may be inefficient for the

---

[7]Kenneth R. Andrews, *The Concept of Corporate Strategy* (Homewood, IL: Dow Jones-Irwin, 1971); R. P. Rumelt, *Strategy, Structure, and Economic Performance in Large American Industrial Corporations* (Cambridge, MA: Harvard University Press, 1974).

diversifying firm, allowing growth without effective control. Diversification increases the opportunities for predatory behavior and allows the concealment of profits that might tempt new entrants.

Vertical integration can bring real efficiencies in reduced production costs, lower costs of transactions, and reduced risk (including risk of oligopolistic instability). Vertical integration increases the risk for unintegrated competing firms and tends to deter new entrants.

The multinational firm can be viewed as one diversified among geographic markets or vertically integrated across a national boundary. Foreign investment to produce the same goods abroad as the investor produces in the home market occurs chiefly in markets for differentiated products, though transportation costs and tariffs are also influential. The influence of multinational firms on their markets is rather similar to that of diversified firms. They are a source of new entrants to protected markets, but they tend to promote nonprice competition and may cause oligopolistic interdependence to stretch across national boundaries.

The extramarket activities of the large firms competing in a market contribute a general element of market structure beyond those already studied. If these extramarket activities are diverse, the firms are likely to find it difficult to reach or sustain an agreement with their rivals, and the market will be more competitive.

# Chapter 4

# Market Conduct

We have mapped the major elements of market structure—concentration, product differentiation, barriers to entry, and several others—which make up the economic environment of firms in an industry. The importance of market structure lies in the way it induces firms to behave. We shall call their behavior in changing prices, outputs, product characteristics, selling expenses, and research expenditures their *market conduct*. Conduct links an industry's structure to the quality of its performance. In fact, market performance is our evaluation of the results of firms' behavior.

## WHAT IS MARKET CONDUCT?

*Market conduct* consists of a firm's policies toward its product market and toward the moves made by its rivals in that market. We do not intend to study all aspects of a firm's behavior here, and the word *market* provides the key to which aspects we will cover. A firm may rearrange the responsibilities of its vice-presidents, but that is an "internal" matter which does not relate to its market behavior—unless the vice-presidents are falling down on the sales job. A firm may make contributions to charity. This is "external" behavior, certainly, but it likewise bears no relation to the market in which the firm sells its product. A market functions to determine the price of a product and the quantity that people choose to buy. It also sets the quality of the product, its style or the range of styles offered, and the type and amount of advertising and other such lures which the firms use to attract customers. The firm not only sets its own tactics but also reacts to those of its rivals until a consistent result (that is, equilibrium) prevails across the entire market. These actions and reactions constitute market conduct. To simplify our study, we shall divide market conduct into three major areas of business policy:

1. Setting prices.
2. Setting product quality and other nonprice policies.
3. Seeking strategic advantage and deterring entry.

## THE SCOPE FOR MARKET CONDUCT

Economic theory tells us that each major type of industry will provide a different scope for firms in choosing their behavior patterns. In some industries the firm may have practically no freedom of action; in others, a great deal.

### Conduct under Pure Competition

Consider an industry that matches the textbook model of pure competition. In terms of the elements of market structure, it would exhibit very low concentration, insignificant barriers to entry, and no product differentiation. In this environment, the individual firm has no significant freedom of choice. The market sets the price for its product, and it cannot profitably ask a different one. The absence of product differentiation means that the firm has no choices to make about the design or style of its product. No problems arise for setting the advertising budget: The firm by assumption cannot differentiate its product and advertises only to inform buyers of its existence. Pure competition even denies the firm any choice about how efficient it will be! If its many rivals keep their costs as low as possible, it can only do likewise or else be forced out of business as a result of subnormal profits.

### Conduct under Pure Monopoly

The pure monopolist is almost as limited in playing an independent hand. One particular combination of price and output is optimal for the profit-maximizing monopolist. There will be some optimal level for the advertising budget, such that the last dollar spent just buys an extra dollar of gross revenue. The "quality level" of the product and the range of sizes and colors in which it comes can all be set by some plan so as to maximize profits. The monopoly's demand and cost curves may shift from time to time in response to changing prices and incomes in the economy, but these shifts merely call for routine corrective actions. It responds only to general economic changes, not to the challenge of some particular business rival. The only real choice for the hypothetical monopoly firm is whether to maximize profit or to pursue some other objective that gives utility to its owners or managers.

### Conduct under Oligopoly

When we turn to the many industries having some tinge of oligopoly, possible patterns of market conduct grow much more complex. The essence of oligopoly is that firms are few enough to recognize the impact of their actions on their rivals and thus on the market as a whole. When one firm cuts its price, it considers the possibility that sales snatched from its rivals may cause them to cut their prices too. This is a distinctive element of market conduct found only in oligopolistic industries. When an industry contains one firm (monopoly) or many firms (pure competition), the individual sellers react only to impersonal market forces. In oligopoly they react to one another in a direct and personal fashion. This interaction of sellers in an oligopolistic market we call *mutual interdependence*. The important thing about this interdependence is that it be *recognized*. When a seller in pure competition raises its output, we expect that the market price will be depressed by a very tiny amount. What makes competition pure is that neither the firm nor its rivals notice the price decline. What makes for oligopoly is that they all notice. If beauty exists in the eye of the beholder, oligopoly exists in the eye of the participant.

We saw in Chapter 1 that many industries in the U.S. economy are moderately concentrated—not monopolies, but with the largest firms controlling enough sales that they could conceivably recognize their interdependence. Therefore we need to give close attention to the forces influencing companies' behavior in an oligopolistic market. Economic theorists, after providing us with simple deterministic models of pure competition and pure monopoly, throw up their hands at oligopoly. They say that it makes the market outcome "indeterminate." This does not mean that every oligopoly's price is determined by the toss of a coin. Rather, the problem is that the outcome of competition among oligopolists can be determined in many ways, and we need a lot of information to know what theoretical model to apply to a given empirical situation. The following approach to the behavior of oligopolists will help us to understand this problem and also to explain the logic of the approach that we take to the study of market conduct.[1]

Because oligopolists may recognize their interdependence in the market, an important reference point is the behavior pattern they will adopt if they can achieve the fullest possible degree of cooperation. The best they can do, as a cooperating group, is to charge the same price and earn the same profit as a single monopolist (assuming their costs are the same), and divide that profit among themselves in some agreed way. We call that outcome *joint profit maximization*. The analysis of actual oligopoly markets can then run in terms of the factors that limit the degree to which firms, while recognizing their interdependence, can actually attain maximum joint profits. With each factor we include an element of market structure that might underlie it.

---

[1]Economic theory in fact emphasizes the limiting case in which the firm has no systematic expectation about its oligopolistic rivals' reactions but still recognizes that its own decision about how much to produce will affect the market price overall.

*1. No agreement on principle.*   A plan for maximizing joint profits requires the parties to settle on a comprehensive plan of action—what profit they are shooting for, and what risks they will take to secure it. The more heterogeneous the bargaining parties are, the less likely is it that they will agree in principle on pursuing the same package of profits and risks. To take an example from Chapter 3, the more divergent the firms' strategies (diversification, vertical integration, and so on), the less likely they are to agree.

*2. No agreement on details.*   The parties might settle on the same goal of joint maximization but have trouble agreeing on all the details needed to implement it. A great deal of information must be exchanged in an atmosphere of shared trust for consensus to be reached on all the necessary market variables. America's legal framework greatly complicates their task by making such agreements illegal, so that they can be reached only under cover or by the very imprecise process of tacit communication. We shall argue (from both theory and evidence) that oligopolists may often agree on price while leaving many other market variables without consensus.

*3. No adherence to an agreement.*   The parties might reach an agreement but not adhere to it, or some sellers might not agree in the first place. As we shall see, the more ambitious and successful the collusive agreement, the greater the temptation is for any one party to cheat (for example, to shade the agreed price a bit and try to steal some business from rivals). Because it is very hard for oligopolists to devise a mechanism for enforcing their agreements, the temptation to cheat becomes an important limiting force. The more numerous the sellers, the greater the chance that some one firm will feel it can successfully cheat on the agreement without being detected or effectively punished.

Our main strategy in studying oligopoly is to assume that oligopolists recognize the gains from joint maximization but may fail partly or wholly to attain it. Suppose that the oligopolistic rivals are fairly numerous, or that they are ill-informed about what reactions to expect from their rivals. For example, the firm increasing its output may hold a market share big enough to recognize that it will depress the market price, but it may have no systematic hunch about how its rivals will react. Out of ignorance, it assumes that they will not react. Economic theory shows that, in this case, the industry's output will be less than that of a competitive industry but will approach it more and more closely as the number of rival producers increases. And the output will be greater than if the oligopolists could collude effectively.

## PRICE POLICIES

In an oligopolistic market, we usually find each firm quoting its own price and changing it in response to new market conditions or to changes made by its rivals. When the product is undifferentiated, this process of adjustment and response goes on very quickly and sensitively. Few purchasers will pay more for the steel or aluminum of one manufacturer than for that of another. When one seller initiates a price change in such a market, the responses usually occur immediately, or else the sellers' market shares will undergo great changes. The moves and countermoves lead quickly to a new market price. By contrast, when the product is heavily differentiated, oligopolists are less sensitive to one another's price changes. The mechanism of response may operate slowly and weakly, if at all.

### How Oligopolists Set Prices

Like any organization that must make complex decisions frequently, businesses follow certain rules of thumb in order to reduce decision making to manageable proportions. They may set a certain normal rate of return on their investment as a target, or use a standard markup added onto their costs to determine the price.[2] Some economists have declared that the use of these rules of thumb proves that large corporations do not seek to maximize their profits, because the rules obviously will not pick the profit-maximizing price every time. But most people would not draw such a sweeping conclusion. A rule of thumb, after all, is only a practical tool for approximating some ideal objective. The "normal" profit or markup sought might well be the most a firm thinks it can earn without attracting entry, or its closest practicable approach to the profit-maximizing price when costs are constantly changing. A business is apt to override a rule of thumb that casts up prices too far off the mark of maximum profits.

The business manager who has decided what price to announce must next consider what responses the firm's rivals will make to it. Here we also face a great variety of actual practices *and* uncertainty about which ones to call "typical," but the essence of the problem shows clearly enough. For example, an oligopoly considers raising its price. If the price now prevailing in the market is too low to maximize the industry's profits, and if all the rivals also raise their prices, then each firm's profits will increase. Conversely, if one oligopolist lowers its own price without the rivals also lowering theirs, it has a good chance to increase its market share and thus its profits. What to do depends very much on how the rivals are expected to react.

We can depict this problem, as the single oligopolist may see it, in Figure 4–1. If only that firm raises its price, the demand for its product will fall sharply as the product becomes a poor buy beside those that its rivals offer. The opposite happens if only that firm lowers its price. The demand curve confronting it will be very elastic, like *DD* in the diagram. On the other hand, if all its rivals change their prices to match any increase or decrease that it initiates, the change will probably not affect its market share. A price cut will raise its sales only to the extent that a lower price in the market as a whole causes higher sales. If all sellers' prices change together, the demand curve facing the individual seller

---

[2]For a review of descriptive studies of pricing see Donald A. Hay and Derek J. Morris, *Industrial Economics: Theory and Evidence* (Oxford, England: Oxford University Press, 1979), Chap. 4.

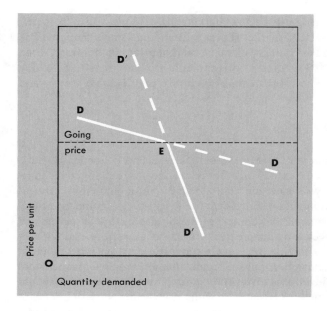

**FIGURE 4–1** The "kinked" demand curve. *DD* is one seller's demand curve when other sellers' prices are unchanged; *D'D'* is one seller's demand curve when all sellers change prices.

will look like *D'D'*. Now, the oligopolist firm may be uncertain whether or not its price change will be imitated by its rivals. It may well be pessimistic about their reactions. It may fear that they will not follow its price increase, in which case its sales volume and probably its profits will fall sharply. On the other hand, it may fear that they will match its price reductions. Its sales volume will then rise by very little, and its total revenue and profits will probably fall. This is a case in which oligopolists may have agreed on a price, but they did not agree on how to change it.

If an oligopolist actually were this pessimistic about its chances of increasing its own profits through a price change, it would view the demand curve that it faces as the solid line *DED'* in Figure 4–1. It would tend to change its price only at rare intervals, when market conditions clearly called for either an increase or a decrease. We call this hypothesis about the reactions that the oligopolist firm anticipates from its rivals the *kinked demand curve*, because of the discontinuity shown in *DED'* at the level of the going price. If all sellers in an industry held this view of their rivals' responses, then the industry price would tend to be rigid, changing only under extreme conditions rather than responding freely to shifts in the conditions of demand and supply. As we shall see in Chapter 5, such pricing patterns have an important implication for the performance of the economy.

We have looked at the process by which a firm selling in a concentrated industry sets its price in relation to its internal costs and the reactions expected from its rivals. Now let us consider how these separately calculated prices of the different sellers are reconciled to yield a consistent industry price.

## How Oligopolists Coordinate Their Prices

*1. Agreement among sellers.*   The most comprehensive means of coordinating prices is a formal agreement among sellers. The agreement may cover nothing more than the price that all sellers will charge for the product.

It may go further and cover selling practices and the quality of the product. It may go further still and carve up markets, allotting a private territory to each seller. The term *cartel* is usually applied to extensive and formal agreements that divide up markets, although no sharp line distinguishes the cartel from less complete agreements.[3]

Attaining maximum joint profits requires a cartel agreement to which all members adhere. Actual cartels have usually been incomplete for the reasons just listed. For instance, sellers who have agreed only on the price that they will charge can nonetheless compete through stepped-up selling efforts and fancier products offered at the fixed price. Price-fixing agreements uncovered in the United States have usually not included all of the competing sellers as members, so that some nonadherence is guaranteed.

In the United States, the antitrust laws discussed in Chapter 6 make cartel agreements illegal in most industries. However, the law enforcers continue to turn up a number of less extensive agreements involving price fixing among competitors and the division of markets, the latter especially in connection with bids for government contracts. The most spectacular price-fixing conspiracy to come to light in recent decades involved the companies making heavy electrical equipment. During the 1950s, their executives met secretly in smoke-filled rooms in hotels across the country to set prices and divide markets.

> The conspiracies in the industry covered such equipment as circuit breakers, power transformers, and turbine generators, which are sold in large extent to power and light companies and government installations. Relatively little product differentiation can be developed among these informed buyers. As a result, a firm's sales depend on offering the best price. Although "book prices" are established for various products, sales are frequently made "off book," and price competition has come to take the form of competing percentages off book price. The cartel agreements were specifically designed to prevent the instigation of price competition, which in some instances had forced prices down to 60 percent of book.
>
> The pattern of the conspiracy can be described by using giant circuit breakers as an example, an item with annual sales of about $75 million in those years. These sales were divided into "sealed-bid" and "open-bid" categories, and the cartel agreement differed between the two. The agreements on sealed-bid business, concluded with public agencies at all levels of government, had the effect of rotating sales on a percentage basis among the participating firms. In the circuit-breaker field, this included at the start all domestic manufacturers. The agreeing firms would determine which one of them would make the low bid in each particular case, and thereby gain

[3]A classic study defined a cartel as "an arrangement among, or on behalf of, producers engaged in the same line of business, with the design or effect of limiting or eliminating competition among them." See George W. Stocking and Myron W. Watkins, *Cartels or Competition?* (New York: Twentieth Century Fund, 1948), p. 3.

the contract, and the price of this bid; and the others would obligate themselves to stay above it. The "open-bid" business was conducted with private utilities, and here the purpose of the cartel was simply the maintenance of established or "book" prices.

It was in the "sealed-bid" category that the conspiracy was the most elaborate. It was here, in the case of switchgear, that the "phases of the moon" formula came into use. The various manufacturers of this equipment were designated by code, and a different one of them was phased into priority to get the business every two weeks. The phasing conformed to the movement of the heavenly bodies. After the low and higher bidders had been determined, there was little evidence that the various firms had not competed freely for the contract.[4]

Like many cartel arrangements, the electrical manufacturers' agreements began because of the desire to maintain prices in the face of strong competitive pressures, but it was precisely these pressures that caused breaks to occur. Periodically, some firm with excess capacity would offer a discount to get a large order. Others would retaliate, and the cartel would lapse. Prices would fall to lower and lower levels, until something had to be done. The cry would go up to stabilize prices, and the meetings would start again. Cartel agreements lacking government sanction may last a long time, but they tend toward recurrent breakdowns, and the ones formed in this industry were no exception. Yet, when in effect, they substantially raised price levels on heavy electrical equipment.

*2. Price leadership.*    Price leadership is a pattern of seller coordination that demands no formal organization among its members. By this arrangement, changes in industry prices are first announced by the "leader," usually the largest firm in the industry. The other firms, the "followers," make the same price changes with little or no time lag. The leader, even when not the largest firm, always holds a substantial share of the market and normally is an old-timer in the industry. Price leadership is most likely in oligopolies selling undifferentiated products. In these industries the sellers' market shares shift drastically if differing prices are charged for the same product.

Patterns of price leadership, like patterns of formal price agreement, vary greatly from industry to industry. The leader may always be followed promptly, or the followers may sometimes delay in matching the leader's change. One leader may always initiate price changes for the industry, or occasionally the role may go to one of the larger rivals. The followers may stick rigidly to their announced prices, or they may occasionally offer "special deals," discounts that might eventually force the leader to make a price cut.

Price leadership by the largest member of an oligopoly has a clear economic logic. The greater a firm's share, the more it has to gain from increased revenue on each unit that it now sells. Looked at the other way, the smaller a firm's share, the more customers it gains proportionally when its reduced price enlarges the market. Therefore, the largest-share firm has an incentive to lead in the sense of setting and

[4]Ralph G. M. Sultan, *Pricing in the Electrical Oligopoly* (Boston: Division of Research, Harvard Business School, 1974), Vol. I; David F. Lean, Jonathan D. Ogur, and Robert F. Rogers, "Does Collusion Pay...Does Antitrust Work?" *Southern Economic Journal*, Vol. LI (January 1985), pp. 828–841.

defending a monopolistic price—or one elevated as close to monopoly as possible without the followers ceasing to follow.

*3. Tacit coordination.* In some industries firms seem able to take one another's responses into account without betraying any external signs as clear as price leadership. Take the case of an industry dominated by a few firms, and with substantial product differentiation. The differentiation removes some of the pressure for uniform prices. Now, suppose that each seller knows that the others will change their "models" at certain regular times and in generally predictable ways. Suppose, also, that every seller knows roughly how each rival calculates and changes its own price in response to changing cost and demand conditions. With this much information, all sellers can independently announce about the same price changes and keep prices at a level yielding some monopoly profits to the industry without any explicit collusion at all.

> The automobile industry nicely fits this pattern of tacit coordination. For decades the "Big Three" (General Motors, Ford, and Chrysler) have used parallel methods of calculating their prices on new models; at the start of each model "season," they independently announce very similar prices for comparable models (for example, four-door family sedans with the least luxurious trim). General Motors generally serves as the price leader, and should another firm find its announced price above GM's benchmark, it cuts back.
>
> The cooperative nature of pricing by the U.S. automakers was highly evident in the early 1980s. The industry had gotten itself into considerable trouble in the 1970s by allowing the quality of its products to slip and by paying little attention to the fast-growing number of imports of higher-quality vehicles (especially from Japan). The "Big Three" restored their fortunes handsomely by getting governmental assistance to restrict the imports and then announcing giant price-hikes on domestic models. (For example, the U.S. Department of Labor calculated that it cost the average family 27.9 weeks of salary to buy a car in 1973, 31.2 weeks in 1979, and 36.6 weeks in 1983.) The "Big Three" apparently decided that maximum joint profits could be obtained, given the state of import competition, by charging much higher prices than before the imports' invasion and settling in the long run for a reduced share of the U.S. market.
>
> These policies were implemented in close parallel by the "Big Three," who justified the price increases to cover their massive investments in cost-reducing technology. That statement is an eyebrow-lifter by itself, even before we consider that each company's most aggressive pricing was on its newest models produced with the latest technology.

## Predatory Pricing Behavior

If rival firms have managed to set a price that yields joint profits, they face the problem of incentives to cheat. Sellers with small market shares or low costs have a lot to gain from defecting, and their rivals with more to gain from preserving the collusion may correspondingly look to strategies for punishing "chiselers." Also, a firm sharing joint monopoly profits may consider the joys of despatching its rival and having all the monopoly gains itself. These incentives raise the issue of predatory pricing, designed to coerce or even eliminate rivals.

One encounters a good deal of popular concern that "big fish eat little fish," and that coercion (or the mere threat of it) by large firms effectively represses small competitors. However, economists are skeptical. To drive out a competitor, even one that is weak or disadvantaged, the aggressor must sacrifice profits now. Profits now are worth more than profits tomorrow. Furthermore, the profits tomorrow (after the rival is gone and the monopoly price established) may be uncertain if new entrants can spring up to replace the victim. The successful predator, therefore, needs some entry barriers to keep itself from being nibbled by replacements. Predation pays best when the predator can send an advance warning signal of its ability and determination to eliminate rivals or sharply curb their market opportunities. If the aggressor can rattle its sabre but not actually use it, the loss of short-term profits can be avoided while the long-term objective is attained.

However commonly or uncommonly markets provide opportunities for predatory strategies, the antitrust laws of the United States take a dim view of many kinds of business tactics aimed at coercing rivals (as we shall see in Chapter 6). As a result, outright cases of predatory pricing to destroy a competitor are probably uncommon, and even in the antitrust prosecutions brought for predatory actions the evidence fails in the bulk of cases to confirm its presence clearly.[5] Signals designed to induce cooperative behavior in oligopoly are no doubt more common, although their effectiveness in shoring up shaky collusive arrangements is limited.

> The U.S. passenger airlines provide examples of apparently coercive price signaling. Airfares are recorded in an integrated industrywide computer network, so they can be changed frequently and at low cost, and the changes observed immediately by rival airlines. Newspaper accounts have shown how a price cut by airline $A$ that directly affects competitor $B$ may be resisted by $B$ with massive if temporary cuts on routes important to $A$.[6]

## Pricing and Market Performance

Pricing behavior sometimes draws a great deal of attention. When a major industry tangles with the president of the United States over a price increase, when the U.S. Department of Justice indicts a group of respected American businesses for conspiring to fix prices, price-making conduct becomes front-page news. We wish to know, therefore, whether the methods of price setting chosen by an industry affect the performance of the economy significantly.

Some patterns of pricing certainly do. Successful collusion can raise profit margins, preserving excess capacity or deflecting resources away from a sector. Oligopolistic patterns of price setting and coordination that make prices rigid (although perhaps not monopolistic) may distort the allocation of resources.

[5]R. H. Koller II, "The Myth of Predatory Pricing: An Empirical Study," *Antitrust Law & Economics Review*, Vol. II (Summer 1971), pp. 105–123.

[6]*Wall Street Journal*, June 28, 1990, pp. A1, A8; October 9, 1990, pp. B1, B10.

On the other hand, we must be cautious about predicting performance from patterns of pricing conduct. Should we expect that the more evidence of price conspiracy we spot in an industry, the more monopoly profits it will earn? The answer is yes, if the agreement commands any sustained adherence from its members. Should we *also* expect that large firms engaging in illegal price fixing earn higher profits than other large firms? One should not be too quick with an affirmative answer. Price fixing is risky. Firms may resort to it only when tacit collusion will not do the trick, or when the industry has suffered some bad breaks. Collusion may stem from desperation more often than from greed: The statistical evidence indeed suggests that large firms caught engaging in illegal collusion earn lower profits than other large firms.[7]

The same problem arises with price leadership. Some economists have regarded price leadership as a means for sellers to designate one of their number to choose the price which maximizes monopoly profits for the industry. Others have held that the price leader only calls the turns of the competitive price, which yields no abnormal profits. Either interpretation might be right for a particular case, because all the appearances that we could observe might be the same.[8]

## PRODUCT POLICIES

The story of pricing patterns in industries with oligopolistic elements covers only a part of their market conduct. Wherever any product differentiation appears, new kinds of decisions must be made about the "quality" of the product and the amount of selling costs expended on it, whatever the price charged. The individual seller asks not only, "Can I raise my profits by cutting my prices?" but also, "Can I raise my profits by raising the quality of my product?" or, "Can I raise my profits by increasing my advertising budget?" The decision in each case flashes a signal to the firm's market rivals. Will they ignore its new and improved product, letting it take a greater market share, or will they respond with changes of their own? Will one seller's stepped-up advertising campaign be matched by its rivals?

### Product Differentiation and Advertising

Some product differentiation must exist for these new dimensions to affect the market conduct of an industry. The structural character of product differentiation sets the general payout to the sellers from their advertising outlays and other expenditures affecting the quality and variety of the goods and services they offer. These relations get rather complicated, so we shall consider how competition affects one particular policy—advertising. Then we can see how other product policies fit in.

---

[7]Peter Asch and J. J. Seneca, "Is Collusion Profitable?" *Review of Economics and Statistics*, Vol. LVIII (February 1976), pp. 1–12.

[8]See Joe S. Bain, "Price Leaders, Barometers, and Kinks," *Journal of Business*, Vol. XXXIII (July 1960), pp. 193–203.

Suppose that you monopolize the production and sale of a popular beverage called "grog." As a profit-maximizer, you contemplate how much your net revenues can be raised by different levels of advertising outlay. Your advertising may shift the demand curve for grog outward by making people willing to buy more at any given price. You profit when people drink more gallons of grog, and your profit increases further as an inelastic demand curve lets you raise the price per guzzle. Still more benefits roll in if the advertising also makes people's demand for grog less elastic. Taking these things into account, you expand your advertising outlays to the point where the last dollar buys you just one more dollar of grog profits.

Now shift the assumption to allow for competing beverages, pop and fizz. Everyone regards them as close substitutes for grog. Whatever the rivalrous relations among the makers of pop, fizz, and grog, assume that they do not collude with one another perfectly. Now a new element enters into determining the best advertising outlay on grog (or pop or fizz). When grog was monopolized, extra advertising by the grog monopolist shifted demand outward by altering people's tastes, causing them to spend less on yachts and shoes and more on grog. But the grog oligopolist's advertising shifts demand in another way as well: People will quench their thirst with grog rather than pop or fizz. Therefore, a noncollusive oligopoly market structure is more likely to yield a higher level of industrywide advertising outlay than would a monopoly market structure.

To test this hypothesis about advertising and competition, we need to know to what extent oligopolists compete openly in advertising, so that their ads merely offset each other rather than expand the demand for the industry as a whole. Statistical methods applied to this rather tricky question have generally confirmed the hypothesis: With other influences controlled, moderately concentrated industries do spend more on advertising than do highly concentrated ones.[9] Investigators generally find that brand A's advertising eats into the market share of competing brand B. A's and B's advertising outlays may do little more than extinguish each other's effect on buyers.

Case studies also reveal the extent of rivalrous advertising in oligopolies. In 1970 the U.S. Congress enacted the Public Health Cigarette Smoking Act, which banned cigarette advertising on radio and television. The cigarette makers had the option of expanding their advertising in less cost-effective media, such as magazines and newspapers. If the sellers had been spending no more on advertising than the sum that would maximize joint monopoly profits, the ban should have both reduced demand and lowered profits. But if it extinguished heavy outlays on rivalrous advertising, the reduction could well have produced a rise in profits. Advertising outlays fell by about 20 percent, but the industry apparently did enjoy a net increase in profits.[10] So oligopolistic rivalry was reduced.

[9]For example, Douglas F. Greer, "Advertising and Market Concentration," *Southern Economic Journal*, Vol. XXXVIII (July 1971), pp. 19–32.

[10]James L. Hamilton, "The Demand for Cigarettes: Advertising, the Health Scare and the Cigarette Advertising Ban," *Review of Economics and Statistics*, Vol. LIV (November 1972), pp. 401–411. The text omits one piece of the story: The advertising ban also took off the airwaves advertising by antismoking groups about the health hazards of smoking cigarettes. With those dismaying facts out of sight, smokers lit up in greater numbers.

Because rivalrous advertising wastes resources, and because heavy advertising outlays can elevate entry barriers in some industries (see Chapter 2), advertising gets panned by some economists. We should recognize, therefore, that outside the familiar consumer-nondurable goods sectors, advertising serves mainly to convey information to prospective buyers: What are the specifications of this camera? Which supermarket has the best price on coffee? Each prospective buyer could get this information by shopping around, but the seller's advertising may well transmit the information more cheaply. We return to the normative significance of advertising in Chapter 5.

## The Range of Product Policies

The evidence on advertising and competition yields some fairly simple conclusions. But what happens when we think about all the other instruments that businesses can use to vary the product they offer and the ways they promote its sale? Price policies are easy to discuss, because all you can do with a price is raise or lower it. But businesses can promote their sales with all sorts of devices. They can advertise directly to the final consumers, using all sorts of advertising media and techniques. They can offer incentives to retailers or other sales outlets in order to promote their products, such as service stations owned by gasoline refiners and leased to operators at low rentals. Policies involving the product itself may show an even wider variety. It can be made more durable or less durable. Optional extras may be made standard equipment, or vice versa. The range of styles or colors may be expanded or contracted. Chrome plate may be added, removed, or rearranged.

How can we think systematically about all these choices that producers make when deciding what products to offer us? It helps to attack the question in two stages. First, put the issue of oligopoly aside, and assume that many producers offer different varieties or brands of some product—each brand with its own distinctive attributes. Assume—this is important—that for each brand its producer must incur a *fixed* cost. Assume also that anybody can enter the market, so that producers will spring up to offer new brands if they can sell enough (at the profit-maximizing price) to cover their fixed costs and return normal profits. Will sellers offer that set of brands or varieties that give the most value to consumers? Your intuitive guess probably goes like this: "Yes, because if entry is free and profits are normal, what can be wrong?" But something may be wrong. Consider Stoopies, a brand bought by relatively few customers but liked very much by some of them. Because some crave Stoopies while most people skip them, the demand for Stoopies is small and price-inelastic. There may in fact be no price that a Stoopies producer could charge that would cover total costs (including the fixed element). Yet some Stoopies freaks get so much utility from consuming the brand that they would potentially be willing to pay enough to cover the producer's costs. Society would then gain if Stoopies were produced, yet the producer may be unable to collect from this minority enough revenue to cover the fixed cost. This is the problem of "product selection," and it tells us that even a seemingly competitive market need not produce the right set of differentiated products.

Oligopoly adds a further complication to the market's performance in selecting nonprice dimensions of the product. Because we are unsure that the market produces the right set of products, even with oligopoly absent, we can say how oligopoly makes things *different*, but we cannot be sure that they get *better* or *worse*. In oligopoly, any nonprice dimension of product can be affected by the intensity of rivalry among the sellers. Suppose at first that they are perfectly collusive and maximize their joint profits. They would offer some set of product varieties and qualities and some amount of sales promotion. But when rivalry provokes competitive moves and countermoves, these nonprice policies change. Product quality may go up. Brands may proliferate. Firms may spend more on sales promotion. Whatever competition does to price, we can identify the direction in which rivalry is likely to push these nonprice dimensions of the "deal" that the seller offers to customers.

Economists' statistical studies confirm that the more rivalrous the oligopoly, the higher the incidence of nonprice competition. As with advertising, they reach this conclusion by comparing highly concentrated oligopolies and near-monopolies, on the one hand, to moderately concentrated markets where tight recognition of mutual dependence is unlikely. Rivalrous oligopolists maintain more excess capacity (to assure serving the customers if demand should peak unexpectedly). In the banking sector they spread more branch banking offices around town. If the industry undertakes multinational activity, the rivals all rush out to start foreign subsidiaries at the same time in the same host countries.[11]

> The cigarette industry, this time in Australia, provides a dramatic instance of product rivalry in the form of "brand proliferation." A monopoly would offer the public a certain choice of varieties or brands, so as to maximize its profits. Rivalrous sellers, however, would expand the number of brands, increasing their costs but potentially raising their individual profits by drawing customers from their rivals' brands. In 1955 the Australian cigarette industry was a monopoly, but four competitors entered in the next ten years. The monopoly had offered five brands, all the same size and selling at the same price. The entrants began offering different types and sizes of cigarette, and by 1967 the total number of brands soared to 128. This number may have been "excessive," but the Australian smoker certainly had more choice than before. Advertising also increased a great deal, rising ten-fold between 1954 and 1961.[12]

### Pricing Conduct and Product Conduct

The majority of industries seem to be more independent (and less collusive) in their product policies than in their pricing policies. Price adjustments, more often

[11]See R. E. Caves, J. P. Jarrett, and M. K. Loucks, "Competitive Conditions and the Firm's Buffer Stocks: An Exploratory Analysis," *Review of Economics and Statistics*, Vol. LXI (November 1979), pp. 485–496; John T. Scott, "Nonprice Competition in Banking Markets," *Southern Economic Journal*, Vol. XLIV (January 1978), pp. 594–605; Fredrick T. Knickerbocker, *Oligopolistic Reaction and Multinational Enterprise* (Boston: Division of Research, Harvard Business School, 1973).

[12]M. A. Alemson, "Advertising and the Nature of Competition in Oligopoly over Time: A Case Study," *Economic Journal*, Vol. LXXX (June 1970), pp. 282–306.

than product adjustments, seem to aim at protecting maximum joint profits for the industry. Some very good reasons for this come to mind.

In an oligopoly, the chances of a seller's acting independently, and without heed to the effect on joint profits, depend on what the firm thinks it can get away with. Can it raise its profits and market share at the expense of its rivals? Will they fail to counter its move, or will they fail to counter it effectively? A price reduction can always be met. If the change is in announced list prices, then rivals learn of it immediately and have only to change their own lists. If the change takes the form of secret and selective cuts to certain buyers, then the news will surely get to rival sellers if it affects enough sales to make a difference. Contrast the results of a change involving any element of product policy. Every action in this field has its elements of uniqueness. Even if rivals bend all their efforts to meet a new product strategy or advertising campaign, they may not succeed. An adroit advertising campaign may induce deep-seated shifts in consumer preferences that no countervailing campaign, even if more heavily financed, can successfully offset. The same holds true for styling innovations in the product itself, especially if the new gimmick can be protected from imitation by means of a patent or copyright. Even if advertising and product strategies can be met by rivals, the time required to mount a counter-attack gives the aggressor an advantageous head start. In short, product strategies are more likely than price strategies to fill the requirements for independent action: The initial move will not be met by rivals. Advertising and product strategies are likely to evade successful regulation by would-be collusive oligopolists, and they contribute to destabilizing market shares and upsetting collusion in concentrated industries.

> The airlines nicely illustrate the relation between price and nonprice competition. An important form of nonprice competition is how much capacity an airline offers on a given route: The traveler prefers a wide choice of departure times and the luxury of the next seat being empty. Up until the late 1970s, changes in airline fares required government approval, and that requirement effectively blocked price competition. Afterward, airlines competing on a route priced as they would. When prices were locked in by regulation, rivalrous markets showed much more excess capacity (lower "load factors") than they did later, after the regulatory floor crumbled and competition occurred in prices as well as load factors.[13]

## COMMITTED COMPETITION AND ENTRY DETERRENCE

The examples in the preceding paragraph suggest an important distinction you should make when you are studying market conduct. Is a particular strategic move reversible? Or, once done, is it irreversible? Price setting is clearly a reversible process. This morning I cut my price in hope of raising the profits I get from the

---

[13]D. R. Graham, D. P. Kaplan, and D. S. Sibley, "Efficiency and Competition in the Airline Industry," *Bell Journal of Economics*, Vol. XIV (Spring 1983), pp. 118–138.

market that we share. Tonight a brick crashes through my window. Tomorrow I restore my price to its former level. Suppose instead that this morning I introduce a new product, the result of my heavy investment in research and development. Even if my window is shattered at midnight, I am unlikely to withdraw the innovation. My development costs *are already sunk*, and to keep the new product on the market I incur only its variable costs of production. By sinking my costs in the competitive move, I commit myself to stick with it. And if you understand that point, you will save your brick for another use. These examples suggest the importance of distinguishing between *committed* and *uncommitted* forms of competition. We shall now consider the implications of committed competition, first among firms already present in the market, then for an incumbent firm hoping to deter entrants.

### Commitment Opportunities and Commitment Races

We have already suggested that nonprice dimensions of rivalry are harder to control among oligopolists than price competition. That is indeed the central implication of commitment opportunities among incumbent firms. Because cutting my price gives me no permanent advantage once you retaliate, we live and let live, avoiding price competition. But we have no such hesitation about snatching any opportunities for competitive moves that involve commitment.

Consider what this means in a clear-cut case. You and I share a "high technology" market in which an important innovation is in prospect. The innovation will be costly to develop, but whichever of us gets it first will obtain a patent and control the whole market. The market is not yet ripe for the innovation. That is, if you were not around and I had a monopoly, I would recognize that the most profitable time to bring the innovation onto the market is in the future. However, if I wait that long, you will preempt me, so I speed up my project and spend more in the hope of beating you out. You, of course, are thinking the same way. We are in a "commitment race" to achieve the innovation and grab the patent. We both speed up, so that whichever of us discovers the innovation will put it on the market at such a time that it will yield only a normal profit, and not the excess profits that a monopolist could have obtained from innovating later (at lower cost and in a bigger market). Thus, in the extreme, it takes only two symmetrical rivals racing to make a commitment to eliminate any excess profits from the market. That is quite different from uncommitted rivalry (day-to-day price setting, for example) in which even a moderately large number of firms may manage to reap some excess profits.

This difference between committed and uncommitted conduct has potentially important implications for market structures and the performance levels that they deliver. Roughly speaking, given the number of sellers, the market should be more competitive as the opportunities for commitment increase. Some economists have suspected that markets rich in commitment opportunities may be effectively competitive even if the incumbent firms are few, entry barriers high, and so on. Recent empirical research does not entirely support this, however; some cooperation among incumbents survives even in markets where long-run conduct is dominated by firms' decisions about expanding plant capacities to serve a growing market. Plant-capacity decisions certainly offer a chance for preemption to the firm that inaugurates a plant that uses frontier technology and exploits all available scale economies.[14] On the other hand, in long-lived, stable industries, incumbents tend to be somewhat cooperative in their investment planning. A study of the chemical processing industries found this pattern: If you expand your plant, I back off with my expansion plans so that we are spared excess capacity. If an entrant builds a plant, however, we react aggressively in our investment plans—hang the consequences for excess capacity.[15]

Committed competition has many other important implications. It can give rise to systematic differences among firms competing head-on in a given market. One firm may make heavy investments in efficient plant capacity in order to become the low-cost competitor. Another may invest in achieving high quality or distinctive style for its product. Each strategy involves committed investments that cannot be reversed, and the lucky firm that makes a timely move gains a sustained advantage that its rivals may be unable profitably to copy or offset—not because they are less adept, but because a strategy that was profitable for the first-mover will become unprofitable for everybody if someone copies it. Rivals know that the first-mover facing competition will not back off from a strategy once its cost is mostly sunk. Writings on business strategy have given much emphasis to this point.[16] As firms press for competitive advantages, diverse strategies may succeed in a given market. We observe competitors who are dissimilar to one another. These strategic differences may make them react differently to disturbances striking the market, so that they have more difficulty sustaining mutual understandings in day-to-day noncommitted forms of competition, such as price setting.

### Entry Deterrence

When we introduced entry barriers in Chapter 2, we stressed their structural underpinnings. However, the conduct of incumbent firms influences actual entry in two ways. First, given the structural barriers to entry, the price and product policies of the going firms determine whether entrants can expect to make a profit, and thus whether or not they enter. Second, the going firms may be able to raise the entry barriers directly. Entry deterrence is another form of committed competition in which the first-mover seeks advantage against potential rather than actual rivals.

Joe S. Bain, who established the concept of entry barriers, measured them by the "limit price"—the most the going firms could charge without attracting entry.

---

[14]For an example of such an attempt to preempt and its consequences for the market, see Pankaj Ghemawat, "Capacity Expansion in the Titanium Dioxide Industry," *Journal of Industrial Economics*, Vol. XXXIII (December 1984), pp. 145–163.

[15]Marvin B. Lieberman, "Postentry Investment and Market Structure in the Chemical Processing Industries," *Rand Journal of Economics*, Vol. XVIII (Winter 1987), pp. 533–549.

[16]Michael E. Porter, *Competitive Strategy* (New York: Free Press, 1980); Pankaj Ghemawat, *Commitment: The Dynamic of Strategy* (New York: Free Press, 1991).

The going firms decide whether to settle for the limit price or to charge more and thus encourage entry. The siren song of the quiet life might tempt incumbents to avoid attracting new rivals. However, a subtler view of profit maximization may point the other way. Going firms that exceed the limit price enjoy the short-run monopoly profits now. The entry that they prompt occurs only after a lag, and so the loss of profits lies in the future and hence gets discounted. Pricing so that entry eventually occurs could therefore yield a greater present value of profits than pricing to keep entrants out.

Subsequent research has attached some qualifications to the limit-price concept. The going firms manipulate many conduct variables other than price, as we have seen, so "limit price" stands for a set of market policies. Also, what determines entry is not the going price but the price that the entrant expects to prevail after arrival on the scene. Going firms would certainly like to charge the short-term monopoly price but signal their intention to cut to the bone if an entrant tiptoes within. They may be able to send such signals. One way is to maintain excess production capacity. The astute would-be entrant then figures that the going firms could cut the price and still take the increased business that the price cut generates, leaving no crumbs for the newcomer.

Incumbents may be able to raise entry barriers directly. Both economic theory and industry case studies suggest many possible ways. Vertical integration can equip the going firms with "squeeze" capability. Or integration into the control of retail distribution can raise absolute-cost barriers for the entrant who must create or mobilize a new set of distribution channels. Even the cost curve that embodies any scale-economy barriers to entering the industry can depend on the going firms' strategies. Suppose that one product policy is to offer a "new model" each year. Suppose that the new model stimulates demand, but that it imposes a fixed cost of design and tooling on the seller. The policy could increase the profits of incumbents who hold large market shares, over which they can spread the extra fixed costs. But it could cut profits for smaller actual rivals and for entrants who must start out small.

> The history of antitrust cases (see Chapter 6) includes a number that document types of entry-deterring behavior. One example is United Shoe Machinery Co., which found many ingenious ways to deny competitors access to its shoe-manufacturer customers. It chose to lease many of its machines rather that sell them, and these leases were long-term and could not be cancelled without penalty. United Shoe Machinery held important patents on some machines, and a shoemaker could not lease these unique machines without taking the "ordinary" ones as well. These policies neatly closed off all strategic options for entrants. They could not easily sell machines to the undercap-italized shoemakers, and hence faced the capital-cost barrier of financing an inventory of rented machines. They could not start by offering just the simple (unpatented) machines because of United Shoe Machinery's tying arrangement. They could not win by offering a better machine than United's specialties, because the long leases would keep many potential customers from promptly switching suppliers.[17]

[17]Carl Kaysen, *United States* v. *United Shoe Machinery Corporation* (Cambridge, MA: Harvard University Press, 1956).

Many business policies that may deter entrants probably do so incidentally while serving innocent primary purposes, as United Shoe's practices probably did. Economists hence wonder to what extent incumbents step up their levels of such policies in order to gain extra benefits from entry deterrence. One investigator simply asked businesses what policies they used more than occasionally to deter entry. Nearly all of his candidate policies drew positive responses from one-fifth or more of the managers. The front runners were advertising, research, filling niches that might attract entrants, and managing reported profits to conceal how lucrative some activities really are.[18]

## SUMMARY

We apply the term *market conduct* to the behavior patterns that firms in an industry exhibit in the market where they sell their product. It arises within the environment of an industry's market structure. Market conduct holds little interest in purely competitive or purely monopolistic industries. Here, firms simply react to the impersonal economic forces around them. In oligopolistic industries, however, firms react to one another, and the consequences grow more complex. The best that a group of cooperating oligopolists can achieve is joint profit maximization—the equivalent to what a monopolist would earn. We analyze patterns of market conduct in terms of how closely they bring an industry to joint maximization.

An important range of conduct patterns centers on determining oligopolistic market prices—that is, the ways in which firms set their prices and change them in response to others. They use assorted rules of thumb in setting prices, and make their pricing decisions in light of how they expect their rivals to react. The kinked demand curve describes one possible set of expectations they may entertain about their rivals' responses. It implies that oligopolistic prices would tend to be rigid. Oligopolistic industries employ various ways to coordinate their pricing decisions in the market: outright price-fixing agreements and cartels, price leadership, and patterns of tacit collusion. It is hard to predict the consequences of these pricing patterns unless we take note of the market structures within which they occur. Predatory pricing may occur as firms seeking to preserve joint-maximization policies launch attacks on those who have defected; they may also attempt to eliminate rivals, although this is both illegal and unlikely to pay off for the aggressor.

Where product differentiation exists, conduct patterns also develop around product changes and sales-promotion policies—the annual model changes and new improved ingredients that we see around us and hear about constantly. Like patterns of price coordination, these can reflect either joint monopoly action by a group of sellers or outright competitive rivalry. The difference is very hard to tell. Firms in many industries seem more concerned about adjusting their product and sales

[18]Robert Smiley, "Empirical Evidence on Strategic Entry Deterrence," *International Journal of Industrial Organization*, Vol. VI (June 1988), pp. 167–180.

policies than their prices, however, because product changes afford a better chance of stealing a march on a competitor before it can react.

Committed conduct involves those policies that are not easily reversed once in place. If the market offers rich opportunities for committed conduct, races among rivals to make the first commitment may eliminate excess profits. On the other hand, the pursuit of commitment opportunities can lead to an industry of heterogeneous firms that have succeeded with diverse strategies, or it can permit an incumbent monopolist or oligopoly group to elevate the entry barriers that protect it from new competitors.

# Chapter 5

# Market Performance

We come to market performance only after a study of market structure and conduct, yet it was to reach this destination that we discussed those topics. We construct economic theories and organize economic facts to find out why things happen as they do, and how they might be made to come out better. We apply the tools of price theory to the markets in the American economy in order to answer the two principal questions of this chapter: How well do our industries perform? What explains the good and bad features of their performance? In the two chapters that follow, we ask how public policy could improve this performance, and we review the policies actually applied to our markets.

## THE MEANING OF MARKET PERFORMANCE

Our economy should achieve four goals if it is to provide the maximum economic welfare for its citizens: (1) It should be *efficient*, employing its scarce factors of production so that they yield the highest possible real income; (2) it should be *progressive*; it should add to its stock of factors of production, raise the quality and variety of the goods it makes available, and improve the techniques with which it organizes factors of production, all at appropriate rates of progress; (3) it should be *fully employed*, because we waste factors of production more by leaving them idle than by using them inefficiently (not to mention the personal hardships that result from unemployment), but this goal should not be achieved through unreasonable inflation of the general price level; (4) it should be *equitable*, distributing its real output among its members to provide for their essential needs and reasonable expectations as well as rewarding their productive efforts.

We define *market performance* as the appraisal of how closely the economic results of an industry's behavior match the best possible contribution it could make to achieve these goals. The following sections of this chapter deal with what economists know about the market performance of American industries and what features of market structure or conduct seem to make it good or bad. This evidence in turn furnishes a basis for passing judgment on our public policy toward industry. Our antitrust laws, our regulatory commissions, our special legislation mitigating competition—all these policies work some change on market performance by shifting either the structure of markets or the behavior of businesses within them. Once we know how these pressures on structure and conduct are likely to affect performance, we have a basis for testing the wisdom of these policies and suggesting possible reforms.

Note that when we speak of good or bad market performance, we are not passing a flat judgment on the American private enterprise system. In providing us with a high standard of living, the system obviously works well in comparison to those of other countries. Our questions here concern the *actual* performance of individual industries, placed beside their *potential*. Can we find gaps in their market performance between the actual and potential? Can we locate reasons for these gaps and suggest ways to eliminate them?

## EFFICIENCY

A primary problem of economic efficiency is how to allocate productive resources among the various types of goods and services produced in the economy. How to apply our scarce economic resources to the unlimited range of uses that they can serve was the first great problem rigorously treated by economic analysis. Indeed, some economists still refer to it as *the* economic problem. The test comes in the satisfaction that resources produce—as measured by the returns which they earn—when used in various ways. If capital earns more in producing apples than oranges, it is a sign that too much capital is engaged in producing oranges. If some capital were to be transferred out of orange groves into apple orchards, the worth to consumers of the extra apples would exceed the value of the foregone oranges. Thus, showing what conditions will produce an even level of profit rates from industry to industry, reflecting an optimal distribution of resources, is a principal concern of industrial organization.

The allocation of resources among industries is not the only aspect of economic efficiency. Profit rates in an industry might be low, not because too many resources are employed there, but because they are combined or used inefficiently. The inefficient use of resources by firms and industries can take any of the following three forms. We do not want firms in an industry to be inefficiently small, so that they are unable to make use of available economies of scale. We do not want industries to carry a large margin of excess capacity at times when the rest of the economy is fully employed, for this excess capacity then becomes wasted capital. Finally, we do not want laziness or inefficiency to burden firms with costs higher than the minimum for whatever outputs they produce. These flaws in the use of resources are due to *technical inefficiency*, as distinguished from the *allocative inefficiency* that results from monopoly.

Still another dimension of the goal of economic efficiency concerns the amount of resources that industries spend on advertising and sales promotion. Advertising has its good and bad points. On the good side, it informs us of the goods available and tells us about market conditions so that we know where to go for the lowest price or the model best suited to our needs. To this extent, advertising makes markets more nearly perfect than they otherwise would be. However, much advertising aims, not to inform, but to misinform us. It seeks to change our preference patterns and create wants that our private introspections might deny. It aims at making us believe statements that may be scientifically unverifiable or false. At the point where advertising departs from its function of informing and seeks to persuade or deceive us, it tends to become a waste of resources. The paper carrying brightly colored ads, the brains wracked to conjure up catchy slogans, these would produce more net satisfaction in other uses. The same sort of argument holds for other types of sales-promotion expenses, some of which inform us, and some of which delude us. It even holds for some of the money that producers spend on differentiating their products from others in the same industry. Are we better off because my fenders are upswept and yours downswept, if neither style affects the car's performance, while each required the use of scarce resources to devise it? No doubt we are both somewhat happier than we would be with a colorless uniformity. But that is not the question. The real issue is whether we feel *enough* better off as a result of a dollar's worth of product-differentiation expenditures to forego willingly an extra dollar's worth of real goods.

### Profit Rates

The notion of "normal profits" as a sign of proper resource allocation lies at the heart of our analysis. The equity capital that entrepreneurs supply to the firms in different industries does the job of balancing business costs and revenues. If entrepreneurs make wrong guesses about the use of resources, their costs tend to run ahead of revenues. They must dip into their equity to make up the difference, and they earn negative rates of return. On the other hand, if they find highly productive uses for scarce economic resources, then their revenues run ahead of costs and they earn high rates of return.

From this reasoning, we conclude that optimal resource allocation—one side of optimal market performance—requires a "normal" rate of return on equity to prevail in each industry. And now comes the first question of fact: what does this normal return amount to in practice? Equity capital comes from the general pool of savings in economy. If not used by entrepreneurs, it could be allotted to any sort of long-term investment. Thus, our problem is to determine the real rate of return to long-term investments in the economy. Variations in the rate of inflation as well as other disturbances make it hard to pin down a specific value. That is because the nominal interest rates quoted in everyday commerce include compensation to the lender for the expected erosion of his capital through inflation. Some economists have guessed that the annual real rate of return on equity capital is around 3 percent, plus the rate of inflation. Alternatively, it slightly exceeds the interest rate on "safe" securities such as government bonds.

The actual profit rate on a particular investment can diverge from the long-term normal rate for several reasons. In a particular year, errors in short-run planning or prediction may lead sellers to under- or over-estimate the demand for their products, and this in turn may yield higher or lower prices or profits than expected. Such deviations in profits from the norm are called *windfalls*. They fill an essential economic function by signaling that plans are being made incorrectly and that reallocations are required. But positive and negative windfalls should about cancel out over the long pull. They should not distort long-run normal profits. Another influence on profits is the risk that entrepreneurs take. The essence of entrepreneurship is bearing economic risks—using capital in ways which might earn either more or less than "safe" investments. Should society pay people for taking these risks? That is, taking all firms in an industry into account—those which yield their entrepreneurs more than would a safe investment, and those which yield less—does the *average* rate have to come out higher than a safe investment in order to keep people playing the game? That depends strictly on how willing people are to take risks. Are they gamblers, ready to take a chance on a big prize, even though the most likely outcome is less profit than on a safe investment? Or do they demand a price for taking chances, in the form of an average return higher than on safe investments? The evidence seems to show that equity capital does demand a somewhat higher rate of return where risks are higher—where firms' fortunes vary wildly, or where profits fluctuate a lot from year to year. Nonetheless, if all firms in an industry regularly earn more than the going return on safe investments, year in and year out, we can hardly attribute the excess to risk.

Profits greater than normal that we cannot lay to risk or windfalls must arise from the one remaining cause: plain, unvarnished monopolistic restriction of output.

A quick glance at the data convinces us that industries earn very different rates of profit. In 1987 and 1988 the larger firms in the tobacco industry earned 21.2 percent after taxes and the pharmaceutical industry 23.2 percent, while the industrial-equipment industry had to content itself with 12 percent and the textiles industry with 11.8 percent. Differences of this magnitude persist for long periods of time.

The variation of profit rates among large industry groups tells us that resource allocation is not all it might be. Furthermore, the evidence points to certain traits of market structure as the source of excessive rates of profit. We would expect from economic theory that high concentration teamed with high barriers to entry would tend to produce high profit rates—concentration by giving firms a chance to garner some of the potential monopoly profits, entry barriers by allowing short-run monopoly profits to be taken without causing entry. Most investigations have found these predictions to hold true. So many forces affect an industry's profits, even over a fairly long period of time, that the level of seller concentration never explains the differences in profits between industries very well. Nevertheless, a number of studies have confirmed that monopoly leads to higher profits. As we go from less concentrated to more concentrated industries, however, profits do not seem to increase steadily. A study using data from before World War II was the first to suggest that a break seems to occur as we reach industries in which the 8 largest sellers control more than 70 percent of sales.[1] Recent studies roughly agree on this threshold. Four-firm concentration probably has to reach about 50 percent (roughly equivalent to eight-firm concentration around 70 percent) before rival firms begin to recognize their oligopolistic interdependence significantly.

To sustain high profits, an industry must also enjoy some protection from entry by new competitors. Drawn from important early studies, Table 5–1 shows average profit rates for two groups of industries classified by both the height of entry barriers and the level of seller concentration. High barriers seem to inflate profits a great deal, compared to situations with medium or low barriers. The table also suggests that the influences of entry barriers and of seller concentration work independently. Given the level of restriction on entry, a more concentrated industry will earn a higher rate of profit. One source of entry barriers—high rates of advertising—has proved particularly controversial. Product differentiation by itself need generate no excess profits for the industry as a whole, as we suggested earlier, but for some differentiated products the advertiser gets a hammerlock on the information sources used by the buyer, and advertised information is subject to scale economies and high absolute costs. *Then* advertising erects a barrier to entry.[2]

**TABLE 5–1**    Average Profit for Industries Grouped According to Seller Concentration and Barriers to Entry

| Level of Seller Concentration[a] | Height of Barriers to Entry | | |
|---|---|---|---|
| | High | Medium | Low |
| 1. Average profit rates for 20 industries, 1936–1940 | | | |
| High | 19.0 | 10.2 | 10.5 |
| Low | —[b] | 7.0 | 5.3 |
| 2. Average profit rates for 30 industries, 1950–1960 | | | |
| High | 16.3 | 11.1 | 11.9 |
| Low | —[b] | 12.2[c] | 8.6 |

[a]High concentration indicates that the 8 largest sellers during the period in question controlled 70 percent or more of sales by the industry; low concentration indicates that the top 8 controlled less than 70 percent.
[b]No industries fell into this category.
[c]Only one industry.

*Source*: Joe S. Bain, *Barriers to New Competition* (Cambridge, MA: Harvard University Press, 1956), Chap. 7; H. Michael Mann, "Seller Concentration, Barriers to Entry, and Rates of Return in Thirty Industries, 1950–1960," *Review of Economics and Statistics*, Vol. XLVII (August 1966), p. 299.

[1]Joe S. Bain, "Relation of Profit Rate to Industry Concentration: American Manufacturing, 1936–1940," *Quarterly Journal of Economics*, Vol. LXV (August 1951), pp. 293–324.
[2]W. S. Comanor and T. A. Wilson, *Advertising and Market Power* (Cambridge, MA: Harvard University Press, 1974).

Research on industrial profit rates has confirmed two more predictions about the influence of market structure. We expect that a high level of *buyer* concentration will slap a ceiling on the profit rates that a group of sellers can earn. The influence of buyer concentration has been detected in the varying degrees of concentration faced by industries selling producer goods.[3] Also, the profits of consumer-goods industries are affected by the market power of the retail channels through which they reach final buyers, and by the importance of those retailers' contributions to the successful differentiation of the manufacturer's product.[4] Finally, evidence supports the proposition developed in Chapter 3 that the more heterogeneous the assets and activities outside the market of the large firms participating in it, the lower industries' profits will be. A study of producer-goods industries concluded that, after seller concentration is taken into account, profits are lower if an industry's sellers show diverse patterns of product-market diversification and vertical integration.[5]

## Efficient Scale of Production

Profit rates reflect market performance in allocating resources *between* industries, testing whether some industries employ too few factors through monopolistic restriction. Other aspects of market performance concern the allocation of resources *within* industries. For instance, most industries seem to contain some plants too small to exhaust all economies of scale. They could be expanded somewhat, and their average unit costs of production would continue to fall. This disadvantage of small scale is frequently not a crippling one. The inefficiently small plant may have costs only a few percent higher than one that has claimed all available scale economies. It may serve a small, isolated region of the country more cheaply than if the goods were shipped a greater distance from a plant of efficient scale. Subject to these qualifications, industrial plants too small to exploit the available scale economies account for 10 to 30 percent of the capacity of those U.S. manufacturing industries that have been studied closely. Once again, an explanation appears in terms of the elements of market structure. Industries with large amounts of inefficiently small capacity seem to be those in which product differentiation holds sway.

> Recent research on the turnover of firms (entry and exit) lends perspective to our concern over suboptimal-scale business units. This turnover is important for competition and efficiency. Most market entrants start out small. Many of them fail quickly, but the ones that succeed grow rapidly, pushing their way into the leaders' ranks, where they may displace and force out the less efficient incumbents. Concern with suboptimal-scale units is misplaced to the extent that small units are transitory participants in this productive, evolutionary process.

[3]S. R. Lustgarten, "The Impact of Buyer Concentration in Manufacturing Industries," *Review of Economics and Statistics*, Vol. LVII (May 1975), pp. 125–132.

[4]M. E. Porter, *Interbrand Choice, Strategy, and Bilateral Market Power* (Cambridge, MA: Harvard University Press, 1976).

[5]H. H. Newman, "Strategic Groups and the Structure-Performance Relationship," *Review of Economics and Statistics*, Vol. LX (August 1978), pp. 417–427.

Since American antitrust laws permit the dissolution of giant firms that have been found to monopolize their markets, we might also ask whether plants and firms in the economy are usually *just* big enough to attain the available scale economies. After all, giant firms frequently consist of many separate plants, each performing the same operations. Can costs be lowered by stringing a number of plants together under the management of the same firm? A study described in Chapter 2 did find significant economies of multiplant operation in two-thirds of the industries that were examined (see Table 2–2). However, firms large enough to exhaust these multiplant economies would still be smaller than the leaders in these industries in the United States.

If up to 30 percent of many industries' capacity lies in plants too small to be efficient, is there also a problem of plants or firms too large to be efficient? To the best of our knowledge, no problem of large-scale inefficiencies exists. Sometimes the largest firm in an industry seems to have higher costs than some of the medium-sized ones. But we can never tell whether these higher costs are an inevitable result of large size, or whether the large firm is just plain inefficient, having let its costs get above the minimum level attainable at that scale.

What traits of market structure decide whether the firms in an industry are efficient, in the popular sense of producing their outputs at the lowest possible costs? This is a frightfully important question, because cutting unit costs can give rise to big gains in economic welfare. We suggested in Chapter 1 that the firm controlled by its managers rather than its owners might divert resources to uses that are inefficient but increase the welfare of the managers. Some studies affirm that inefficiency, because owner-controlled firms earn higher profits than manager-controlled firms having about the same market power.[6] However, one is jumpy about that conclusion, because manager-controlled firms of a given size are also older and have run through the special strengths or unique assets that brought success to the original owners; we expect them to be less profitable for that reason alone.

Research has recently uncovered some factors that determine the gap between average and best-practice productivity performance in U.S. manufacturing industries. Moderately concentrated industries beat either atomistic ones or tight-knit oligopolies. International competition and modern capital equipment both help, while the diversification of large enterprises seems to hurt.[7] Other evidence (from Great Britain) shows that price-fixing agreements nurture inefficiency. As a result, when they became illegal in Britain, their abandonment typically led to both large declines of prices and the demise of some firms—presumably those unable to stand the rain of competition after the collusive umbrella was folded.[8]

[6]J. Palmer, "The Profit-Performance Effects of the Separation of Ownership from Control in Large U.S. Industrial Corporations," *Bell Journal of Economics and Management Science*, Vol. IV (Spring 1973), pp. 293–303.

[7]R. E. Caves and D. R. Barton, *Efficiency in U.S. Manufacturing Industries* (Cambridge, MA: MIT Press, 1990).

[8]Jack Downie, *The Competitive Process* (London: Duckworth and Co., 1958), Chap. 4; D. L. Swann et al., *Competition in British Industry* (London: George Allen and Unwin, 1975), Chap. 4.

## Sales Promotion and Product Changes

If we know the shape of the cost curve for firms in an industry, then figuring out how much of the industry's capacity lies in units of efficient scale becomes just a matter of arithmetic. For some other features of market performance, however, we have no such peg on which to hang our appraisals. We might give an industry poor marks for performance if it spends too much on noninformative advertising. But how much is too much? We might scowl at an industry that inflates the cost of its product by too frequent, trivial design changes. But how frequent is too frequent? We can collect some numerical evidence on these activities, but no one can determine objectively whether they represent good or bad performance.

Some industries spend more than 10 percent of their sales revenues on advertising. Advertising that provides information to the public is not a waste of resources, because buyers have to inform themselves somehow about the goods and services offered in the market place. The cheapest way to inform the buyer may be for the seller to advertise and roll the cost of the ads into the price of the product. But the same industries that spend so much on advertising convey little specific information in their ads. Even so, some economists excuse these outlays because the ads offer the buyer a guarantee of quality that otherwise cannot be detected before purchase. Would I spend a bundle advertising my grog if it tasted so awful that you'd never buy it a second time? Unfortunately, the answer is that I might do just that, if I could cut my costs enough by making cheap grog rather than the real stuff. You'd only try it once, but that would give me my profit!

The problems with uninformative advertising do not stop here. In general, the same industries that produce mounds of uninformative advertising are the ones in which advertising gives rise to entry barriers. The information content varies among advertising media, tending to be high in local newspapers and specialized magazines, low in nationwide television. Yet there is some evidence that advertising outlays giving rise to excess profits, presumably by creating barriers to entry, are only those on nationwide television.[9] Perhaps this advertising should be restricted. Economists kindly disposed to advertising point out in rebuttal that competition is clearly impaired in those markets where advertising is forbidden completely (by the government, or by agreement among the trade). The newcomer to a market cannot wield any competitive effect without some informational outlay to make its presence known. These points are well taken. But to say that some advertising is desirable does not make all advertising desirable.

When firms in an oligopoly compete for sales by means other than changing their prices, they have a wide range of tactics to pick from. Advertising is one of these. Another, closely related, is that of varying the product itself. As we saw in Chapter 4, product rivalry can cover a great range of strategies—stretching (or cutting) the durability of the product, increasing (or decreasing) the range of styles or models offered, raising (or lowering) the frequency of model changes. Each of

[9]M. E. Porter, "Interbrand Choice, Media Mix and Market Performance," *American Economic Review*, Vol. LXVI (May 1976), pp. 398–406.

these moves affects the cost of the product. Each move also affects the value of the product to the typical consumer. And so we have another possible norm for market performance. How long should a light bulb last? Suppose that the 89-cent bulb we buy at the store burns out after 6 months. Suppose that its probable service life could be doubled at the cost of only 2 cents more per bulb. The extra life would be worth 89 cents to consumers, but the extra cost in scarce resources used up would be only 2 cents. Not enough resources are devoted to making light bulbs durable.

What market structures will short-change us on durability or product quality? An old popular suspicion holds that monopolies deny us the everlasting lightbulb, the auto that runs on water, and so on, in order to enlarge their own profits. Economic theory casts doubt on this proposition. The monopolist has exactly the same incentive as members of a competitive industry to sell you the lightbulb with the most cost-effective durability; the difference is that the monopolist charges you the monopoly price for it. In the short run, however, the monopolist who invents a more durable bulb may not introduce it as soon as an entrant who has no stake in the plant tooled to produce the previous model.

We can identify this problem of market performance, but we cannot really score industries on how well they do in product performance. Various industries have been suspected of making their products less durable than would be optimal. The model changes of the consumers' durable-goods industries have also been widely attacked, with people feeling that they use up resources in retooling costs and the like without improving the "real" utility of the product for the user.

## PROGRESS, RESEARCH, AND INNOVATION

Turning to the goal of a satisfactory rate of economic progress, we find on the one hand general agreement that the level of seller concentration has some influence, but strident debate on the other over the direction of that influence. The argument that rapid technical advance requires some degree of monopoly stems originally from the writing of Joseph Schumpeter. He saw the "fundamental impulse" of economic progress to be "the perennial gale of creative destruction," in which old forms of organization and production are destroyed in the creation of new ones. Competition based on price and quantity does not really count, but instead "the competition from the new commodity, the new technology, the new source of supply, the new type of organization—competition which commands a decisive cost or quality advantage and which strikes not at the margins of the profits and the outputs of existing firms but at their foundations and their very lives."[10] In order to bring about these massive innovations, Schumpeter felt that firms had to be protected by some degree of monopoly—to have some room to maneuver.

Other economists point out, though, that one of the strongest incentives to innovate is to get ahead of your competitors. The small competitor who innovates can cherish hopes of becoming a monopolist, if its innovation is wildly successful,

---

[10]Joseph A. Schumpeter, *Capitalism, Socialism, and Democracy*, 3rd ed. (New York: Harper, 1942), p. 84.

whereas the monopolist is already in that position. The leading seller in a concentrated industry has a successful market position and therefore something to lose if the leader should launch an innovation that fails; the pure competitor has no excess profit to give up and no such inhibition. Competition therefore gives sellers the stronger incentive to devise innovations and put them on the market.

These arguments conflict, and we cannot easily tell which rests on the more plausible assumptions. Also, they are hard to apply to actual market structures. Schumpeter says that pure competition does not contribute to progress. The counterargument says that pure monopoly does not, either. But what about all those market structures in between? What of having a little more oligopoly, or a little less? There, the economic theorists are silent.

The Schumpeter hypothesis poses a troubling prospect—that progressiveness may be inconsistent with efficiency, that the competitive market structures required by the latter may actually impede the former. Must we sacrifice efficiency to get progress, or vice versa? It is crucially important to examine the evidence to see whether we have to face a conflict between these two areas of market performance. We have seen that less oligopoly and lower entry barriers would lead to greater efficiency. Is Schumpeter's implication correct that more concentration would increase innovation and progress? Is it true that a medium-sized firm is more likely to be progressive than a very small one? Is it *also* true that a giant is to be preferred to a firm of medium size?

### Size, Concentration, and Progressiveness

In the last two decades, economists have worked hard to supply answers to these important questions. The results are not simple, and so we must follow the details closely.

First let us consider the amounts that large and small firms spend on research and development (R & D). It appears that larger firms are considerably more likely than small ones to engage in research and development. Of manufacturing firms with more than 5,000 employees, over 90 percent maintain research establishments. For firms employing from 1,000 to 5,000, the proportion drops to 56 percent. For small firms it is no more than one-fifth. However, among companies performing research and development, rates of privately financed spending do not clearly increase with the size of the firm. True giants employing 25,000 persons or more spend around 3.9 percent of sales on R & D, while small firms that undertake research spend almost as much (3.7 percent). Middle-size firms' ratios of R & D to sales average about one-third less.

Of course, levels of research activity vary greatly among industries, just as do the sizes of their typical firms. Therefore we should analyze the relation between R&D and firm size industry by industry. In most industries (71 percent), ratios of R&D outlays to sales (for those firms that undertake research) are about the same for small and large businesses. Large units outperform small ones in 20 percent, underperform them in 8 percent of industries.

The impression remains that large firm sizes foster R&D performance in only a minor fraction of U.S. manufacturing industries. Perhaps, however, the advantage of large firms lies not in the amount they spend on research but the numbers of innovations that they discover with those inputs. But how can we compare the diverse innovations that firms bring to market? Investigators have tried two strategies for measuring research productivity:

1. *Patents* issued to different firms provide some evidence of their outputs of innovations. When patents obtained by firms are related to their sizes within industries, the pattern is similar to that for R&D expenditures. Large and small firms do equally well in 73 percent of industries, large firms excel in 11 percent, and small firms in 15 percent. If anything, the research productivity of small firms is a little better.

2. *Important innovations* can be identified by people knowledgeable about an industry's products and technology. Studies of the sources of important innovations have repeatedly given small firms good marks. For example, between 1953 and 1973 U.S. manufacturing companies with fewer than 1,000 employees accounted for 47 percent of important innovations but only (in 1963) 41 percent of employment. The small-firm sector does better in the United States, however, than in other industrial countries.[11]

Although large firms do not dominate the innovative process, the absence of intense competition could still favor innovation, as Schumpeter suggested. There is a positive simple correlation between progressiveness and concentration in manufacturing industries. After all, many industries with numerous small competitors employ simple, static technologies and do little innovating. But are they unprogressive because they are competitive, or because their technologies simply offer little opportunity for scientific advancement? F. M. Scherer was the first to find that, once technological opportunity is controlled, the most concentrated industries no longer appear the most progressive. Instead, moderately concentrated industries (four-firm concentration around 50 percent) are the most progressive.[12] His conclusion has been replicated by a number of other investigators.[13]

> The aluminum industry illustrates nicely the relationship between seller concentration and progressiveness. Alcoa held a monopoly position during the period prior to World War II. In 1945 government policy in selling United States–built wartime plants facilitated the entry of Kaiser and Reynolds, and these have been joined since by several more firms. In this process, the prewar monopoly was transformed into a postwar oligopoly. A study examined technical progress during the two periods and concluded that the reduction in seller concentration was responsible at least in part for increased progressiveness. Despite the fact that Alcoa is considerably larger than its two major rivals, it has not generated industrial inventions at a faster rate. Furthermore, the existence of several producers has led to competitive marketing, increasing the pressures to develop new alloys and new uses for aluminum, including many consumer products, such as foil. Reduced concentration appears to have provided a significant competitive stimulus to innovation.

[11]F. M. Scherer, *Innovation and Growth: Schumpeterian Perspectives* (Cambridge, MA: MIT Press, 1984), Chap. 11.

[12]F. M. Scherer, "Firm Size, Market Structure, Opportunity, and the Output of Patented Inventions," *American Economic Review*, Vol. LV (December 1965), pp. 1126–1150.

[13]Scherer later found (*Innovation and Growth*, Chap. 13) that research-intensity does increase steadily with concentration in industries with low levels of technological opportunity, where an innovator may have the greatest need for freedom from imitators.

Can we draw any conclusions from these findings about the market structures best suited to innovative performance? They do not support a general case for the betterment of innovative performance by combining small firms, in order to have larger firms and more concentrated industries. In the more progressive industries, levels of concentration low enough to secure good allocative efficiency do not seem to conflict with securing good innovative performance. If a conflict between efficiency and progressiveness exists anywhere, it may be in industries where innovative potential is low in any case.

Economists reviewing the evidence have argued even more specifically that innovative performance benefits from fairly unconcentrated industry structures with diverse sizes of firms. To see why, we need to distinguish the stages in which an invention comes into use. Invention itself is in most cases not a large-scale or extremely costly process. Many important inventions have originated outside the large corporate labs in small firms or by independent inventors. The more costly phase is innovation, bringing the invention to the point where it can be placed on the market. There the large, well-heeled firm comes into its own, and we should probably repress our sorrow over the common sight of a small firm, unable to finance the development of its invention, being bought out by a large company. The large firm usefully applies its cash and various knowledge assets to developing the invention, but it also may bring bureaucratic caution if it lacks aggressive rivals.

The final stage is the diffusion of an innovation from the first firm to introduce it successfully to all others that can profitably use it. The evidence definitely indicates that diffusion proceeds faster in more competitive industries. Putting these conclusions together, we might further conclude that the industry structure yielding the best innovative performance contains a mixture of firms—some large enough to pay the bills for a research establishment but with the incentive of strong competitors (and limited entry barriers) to bring innovations to the market and make the diffusion process proceed at an optimal rate.

### Entry Barriers and Technical Advance

Established firms, even within young and progressive industries, are frequently backward about radically new innovations. They tend to be conservative in approach and relatively unreceptive to totally new ideas, especially before they have been completely tested. Thus, neither Bell Telephone nor General Electric, established firms in the communications industry, was interested in the new invention of radio. Many bluebloods of American industry disclaimed any interest in developing the newly invented photocopying machine. Similarly, Alcoa would not invest in a radically new but highly efficient type of ore carrier until it had been proved effective by Reynolds, a newcomer to the industry. Innovations that promise great advances require, in a great many cases, the establishment of a new firm. Moreover, evidence suggests that a large proportion of industrial births are founded on prospects engendered by a new product or process. High entry barriers may well shut off this form of progress, and we might expect low barriers to hasten the pace of technical change. The rise of venture capital firms to support innovative entrants is thus a welcome development.

The absence of entry barriers may also stimulate progressiveness by another route. Easy entry normally strengthens competitive pressures on existing firms. In some cases, these pressures may result in lower prices. In others, firms will react by undertaking research and attempting to accelerate the pace of technical change in order to outdistance any potential rivals. For instance, competition through research has prevailed in the pharmaceutical industry, where it developed from the industry's experience with the original antibiotics during the early postwar years. There was little differentiation of these products and low barriers to entry. New firms entered the expanding market and prices declined sharply. One hundred thousand units of penicillin, which sold for $20 in 1943, fell to 4 1/2 cents by 1950. It was thus made clear to industry leaders that future profits depended on extensive new product introduction. New products would keep the industry from settling down to competition on standardized commodities and hinder the growth of price competition. By emphasizing the improved quality of new products, a sizeable measure of product differentiation was achieved, and producers obtained substantial control over the prices of their products. The establishment of research laboratories was a necessary cost of rapid product introduction and the concomitant development of product differentiation. In this fashion, the competitive pressures stimulated by easy entry pushed the pharmaceutical industry into large-scale research and development activities.[14]

## FULL EMPLOYMENT AND PRICE STABILITY

We normally consider full employment and price stability to be the responsibility of macroeconomic fiscal and monetary policy, so that the achievement of these goals might seem unrelated to the structures of markets. However, seller concentration and the other sources of market power may affect both the flexibility of prices and the stability of output and employment. Economists and others have been embroiled in a long controversy over the effect of industrial concentration on prices. They have fought over two issues:

1. Do concentrated industries raise their prices faster than others and thereby contribute to inflation? This charge seems rather unlikely when we reflect on the message of economic theory. The *level* of price should be higher in a market controlled by a monopoly than in the same market organized competitively. But once the profit-maximizing price is set, the monopolist has no incentive to raise it further. The long-run rate of price increase has actually been less in the more concentrated manufacturing industries, but that is simply because of their greater potential for technical advance (mentioned earlier). Productivity growth causes an industry's price to rise less rapidly than the costs of its inputs, or even to fall. But we cannot rule out the possibility that concentrated industries sometimes push up prices when they have not realized all the monopoly profits potentially available and see a chance to do so.

[14] The industry's development is traced by Peter Temin, *Taking Your Medicine: Drug Regulation in the United States* (Cambridge, MA: Harvard University Press, 1980).

not realized all the monopoly profits potentially available and see a chance to do so. It appears that during the 1950s powerful oligopolies, with a boost from their equally powerful trade unions, took the lead in pushing up the price level. The automobile industry in the 1980s is a prime example.

2. Do prices of concentrated industries move differently over the business cycle from those in competitive industries? Our analysis in Chapter 4 suggested that oligopolies' prices might be sticky; if so, they would fluctuate less over the cycle than those of competitive markets. The kinked-demand-curve hypothesis also suggests that oligopoly prices stay put until a substantial disequilibrium exists, and so we expect changes in their prices to lag behind those of competitive industries. During a period of high inflation, such as the 1970s, the kinked-demand hypothesis falls down because all industries' money prices are changing. Statistical evidence from the 1960s and before tended to support the hypothesis, especially the lag of oligopolies' price adjustments behind competitive industries'. However, recent research has tended to shift the blame from shaky oligopolistic interdependence to long-term contracts in markets where buyer-seller relationships tend to be "sticky."

If oligopolies' prices are more stable than those of competitive industries over the business cycle, oligopolies' outputs should be less stable. This proposition comes straight from economic theory. Think of the effect of general business fluctuations on an industry as shifting its demand curve to the left in a recession, then to the right in a boom. If a concentrated industry keeps its price fixed over the cycle, its output and employment will fluctuate by a certain amount. But when a competitive industry's price falls in the recession, the decline in its output is mitigated; and when it rises in the boom, the increase of its output is dampened. Hence the competitive output should be less unstable. Most studies do show that employment is less stable in the more concentrated industries.[15]

We also have evidence on the stability of investment in concentrated industries. Some economists have argued that concentration might stabilize investment, because firms with market power can take the long view and use their ample liquidity to invest during the recession in productivity improvements or the added capacity they will need in the next upswing. On the other hand, the follow-the-leader habits of oligopolists also suggest that their investment rates might be unstable— either everybody expands, or no one does. The statistical evidence strongly declares that concentration goes with instability of investment.[16]

## SOCIAL DIMENSIONS OF MARKET PERFORMANCE

Equity in our economy requires that individuals be treated fairly. Perceived unfair treatment may be associated with market structures in several ways. Concentrated industries may worsen the distribution of income and wealth. And discrimination

[15]Robert M. Feinberg, "Market Structure and Employment Instability," *Review of Economics and Statistics*, Vol. LXI (November 1979), pp. 497–505.

[16]F.M. Scherer, *Industrial Market Structure and Economic Performance*, 2nd. ed. (Chicago: Rand McNally, 1980), pp. 371–74.

among employees and alienation of workers may show systematic relations to the structures of markets.

## Income Distribution

Concentrated industries protected by entry barriers, we found, tend to charge high prices and earn excess profits. They could worsen the income distribution in two ways: if poor people have more of a taste than the wealthy for the outputs of the monopolized sectors, or if the wealthy claim a larger share of monopoly profits than they do income from other sources. The former connection does not seem important: There is no evident relation between industries' market structures and the place of their outputs in households' consumption patterns.

That monopoly profits go into the hands of the wealthy seems obvious on first glance, because the wealthy derive much larger proportions of their income from dividends on equity shares than do lower-income groups. We must remember, though, that not everybody owning shares in a firm with monopoly power earns a monopolistic rate of return. Even if General Motors earns more than a normal rate of return, the widow who owns a share of GM stock probably does not earn an above-normal return on her investment. If she bought her share recently, she had to pay the going price for it in the securities markets, a price that has been bid up until the share's dividend yield gives only a normal return on its market price. Only if the share was bought before GM achieved above-average profits could we reasonably say that she receives a monopoly profit.

The really major connection between monopoly and the distribution of income arises because the entrepreneur who founds a successful monopoly acquires a large lump of wealth. The founding family can capitalize the future profits of the monopoly by selling stock in the company to the general public, who bid competitively for claims to the expected future monopoly profits and leave the family with a fortune whose value is liberated from the fates that actually befall the company in the future. These lumps of monopoly-derived wealth decay slowly due to inheritance taxes and other forces, but a large fraction of the wealth held by the richest families today may result from this legacy of monopolies formed in the past. It was estimated that the share of personal wealth held in 1962 by families with net worths in excess of $450,000 in today's prices would have been reduced by one-half if no monopolies have ever been formed.[17]

## Discrimination by Race and Sex

Market power may also increase the amount of discrimination against employees on the basis of race and sex. Suppose that employers prefer not to work with members of a certain group. They express this prejudice economically by

[17]W. S. Comanor and R. H. Smiley, "Monopoly and the Distribution of Wealth," *Quarterly Journal of Economics*, Vol. LXXXIX (May 1975), pp. 177–194.

excess profits, discrimination is economically feasible for it. Managers can trade off some profits to increase their own utility by discriminating, just as they can trade them off for faster growth or a larger-size company (see Chapter 1).

Can the employer in a purely competitive industry do the same? Suppose that minority-group workers command a lower wage for a given job than do members of favored groups. If *all* employers in the competitive industry discriminate to the same extent, discrimination raises the unit costs of all firms in the same proportion. The industry's price is elevated, and discrimination remains economically viable because the discriminating firms can cover their costs. But an opportunity exists for any competitive employers who are free of prejudice, because they can hire low-wage minority-group members and attain lower production costs than the discriminating employers. Blessed with lower costs they can expand their outputs, eventually depressing the product's price and inflicting losses on the high-cost employers who discriminate. Therefore we expect competitive industries to display less discrimination than concentrated industries with access to excess profits.[18]

Our factual evidence on market power and discrimination at this stage is unclear because the research studies give conflicting results. Across broad classes of jobs there appears to be discrimination against both blacks and women in industries where firms enjoy market power. On the other hand, studies concentrating on the administrative and professional employees of large companies have found no such effect. The question remains open.[19]

### Worker Alienation

Economists have shown interest in the popular concern that workers in some plants or companies are dissatisfied with their jobs. Boredom with repetitive tasks, ire over supervision by a faceless bureaucracy are negative factors in the real income provided by our economy. If these debits are somehow connected to market structures, they should join our roster of market-performance dimensions. Sociologists and psychologists, who have performed most of the research on worker dissatisfaction and alienation, conclude that people express less satisfaction with their jobs when they work in large plants or are supervised by remote bureaucracies in big companies. But they also get paid more to do the work. This pattern suggests that large workplaces make more effective use of labor, but employees rationally demand more pay to work in less congenial environments. The most recent research,

---

[18]You should note that this analysis depends on the employer's being the only economic agent who is prejudiced. If employees in the preferred group resist working with minority-group members, the enterprise's productivity is depressed by hiring the latter, and the unprejudiced employer would have to discriminate in order to minimize costs. The employer would also discriminate if the firm's customers are prejudiced and willing to pay less for goods and services supplied by minority-group members.

[19]For example, W. G. Shepherd and S. G. Levin, "Managerial Discrimination in Large Firms," *Review of Economics and Statistics*, Vol. LV (November 1973), pp. 412–422; W. S. Comanor, "Racial Discrimination in American Industry," *Economica*, Vol. XL (November 1973), pp. 363–378.

however, has not confirmed that job quality decreases with establishment size, raising a puzzle about why larger units so often pay higher wages. Monopoly rents captured as wages may supply part of the answer.[20]

## SUMMARY

The performance of an economy can be measured along four major lines: efficiency in the use of resources; progressiveness in enlarging and improving the flow of goods and services; stability of prices and employment; and fairness in the treatment of individuals. We define *market performance* as an industry's actual contribution relative to its potential to the achievement of these goals.

The structures of industries clearly affect their efficiency: the allocation of resources between industries, the organization of production in plants and firms of efficient size, and the devotion of a sensible amount of resources to advertising and sales promotion. High concentration of sellers and high barriers to entry jointly tend to support persistently high profits, the signal that resource allocation has gone wrong. The American economy seems to have no major problems of firms that are too small to be efficient in the more concentrated industries, except where product differentiation is heavy. Technical inefficiency, the gap between average and best-practice productivity, is greater for highly concentrated and very unconcentrated industries than for those with middling concentration. The large sums lavished on advertising in part supply us with useful information, but in part serve to create contrived differences among brands and to raise entry barriers to new firms.

As to progressiveness, we know that large firms in general carry on more research than small ones, but in those industries where most of the research takes place, the "giant" seldom does more than its larger rivals. Large firms can undertake costly and time-consuming development processes, but small firms and competitive market structures may be better for generating ideas and putting innovations into use. Neither pure monopoly nor pure competition promotes the most progressive behavior.

Concentrated sectors may sometimes contribute to the problem of inflation by going for a larger slice of their potential monopoly profits. In the main, though, their prices are sticky and tend to rise later in a boom than the prices of unconcentrated industries. If concentrated industries' prices are more stable, their outputs should be less stable than those of competitive industries. The evidence has been mixed, but we do find that the investment of rates of concentrated industries are less stable over time.

Monopoly contributes to an unequal distribution of income, because many of the lumps of wealth held by the richest families come from monopolies that have been created some time in the past. Economic theory suggests that concentrated

[20]Charles Brown, James Hamilton, and James Medoff, *Employers Large and Small* (Cambridge, MA: Harvard University Press, 1990).

Monopoly contributes to an unequal distribution of income, because many of the lumps of wealth held by the richest families come from monopolies that have been created some time in the past. Economic theory suggests that concentrated industries may engage in more discrimination against minority-group employees; some, but not all, of our factual evidence supports that conclusion. Workers in large plants and firms tend to express less satisfaction with their jobs, but the market lets them choose between less satisfying but more productive (and remunerative) work places and those yielding more pleasant environments but less output and less pay.

# Chapter 6

# The Promotion of Competition
## and
## the Control of Monopoly

Market structure and conduct do affect performance. On the evidence from Chapter 5, you could build a case for restricting some forms of market behavior and changing some elements of market structure that impair the performance of American industries. The federal and state governments apply many policies that affect market structure and conduct, apparently with the aim of improving market performance. As we survey these policies and their enforcement, we shall consider how consistent they are with the findings of economic analysis.

## LAWS AND THEIR OBJECTIVES

Economists can state clearly enough their reasons for thinking that some reform or regulation might improve the performance of the economy. They oppose situations of monopoly because they signal an inappropriate use of society's scarce productive resources; monopoly profits stem from restricting the flow of resources into the monopolized sector. Public policy, the result of many voices and many minds, living and dead, carries no such "official" rationale to explain what it seeks to accomplish. Indeed, almost any major economic policy of the United States numbers some strange bedfellows among its regular supporters. Nonetheless, most of the major policies directed toward competition and monopoly in the United States make some sense in terms of economic analysis.

As a useful shortcut, we can describe economic policies "to prevent monopoly and promote competition," on the one hand, or "to prevent competition and promote monopoly," on the other. The nation is most famous for, and proud of, policies falling in the first class. The statute books, however, contain plenty of both kinds. If we could imagine all possible policy measures properly located along a line stretching from "promoting competition" to "promoting monopoly," those actually in force in America would lie at various points along the line, as well as some at either end.

The state of antitrust policy after the 1980s can be described as restless. The federal government moved to relax antitrust policy on several fronts, and court decisions were hostile in some areas. Some antitrust statutes went largely unenforced. Still, the policy had important effects in the past, and it continues to set significant ground rules for competitors in U.S. industrial markets.

It will help to distinguish carefully between policies that aim at the *structure* of industries and those that focus on their *conduct*. A policy requiring the dissolution of firms that have come to hold too large a share of their markets seeks to change market structure in a "more competitive" direction. Likewise, a policy of preventing mergers that would result in a high level of seller concentration affects market structure, but in a *preventive* rather than *curative* manner. On the other hand, a law forbidding agreements among firms to fix prices rules out one form of price coordination between rival sellers, and thus affects market conduct. A ban on selling temporarily at very low prices to drive a competitor out of business would control market conduct, even though the concern is with a sort of conduct that may bring about an undesirable change in market structure.

Identifying policies with market structure and conduct should help us to predict the effects of policies. We possess evidence on the quality of market performance that the different structures and conduct patterns tend to produce. Knowledge of what structure and conduct are promoted by which policy lets us infer how the statutes are in fact likely to affect performance.

## BACKGROUND TO FEDERAL ANTITRUST LAWS

The first major piece of federal law designed to preserve or promote competition, the famous Sherman Act of 1890, grew out of an unusual period of American economic history following the Civil War when "monopoly versus competition" as a question of economic policy first came to the fore nationally. A steadily improving network of transportation and communications was then drawing the United States together economically. Most firms previously sold in local markets, protected from distant rivals by high transport costs. Now, the decline in transport costs and the rapid spread of information were throwing more and more firms into open competition with one another. At the same time, technology was changing rapidly in many industries. Complex new types of machinery were calling forth larger plants and firms than before and were threatening older, smaller enterprises with extinction.

These powerful trends naturally led business managers to search for ways to soften the resultant competitive pressure. They found many. Some sellers agreed to fix prices, divide up markets, share industry profits among themselves, or otherwise eliminate competition. Others merged with or bought out their competitors in order to raise the level of seller concentration. One device used to raise concentration was outright consolidation of dozens of firms into one giant combine. Another was the trust, a legal device for putting independent firms under a common control. To form a trust, majority stockholders of a number of independent companies turned over their shares, carrying voting control over the affairs of their companies, to a single group of "trustees." They received in return trust certificates entitling them to share in the profits of the companies operated by the trustees as a group. The trustees could then run the formerly competing firms as a single enterprise, extracting whatever monopoly profits might be available. The trust device waned by the turn of the century, but not before giving its name to a whole branch of public policy. Similar to the trust was the holding company. It likewise centralized voting control over a number of operating companies in the hands of a single enterprise, and was easier to organize than a trust.

### Sherman Act of 1890

The rise of these types of combinations in industry after industry was mirrored in public hostility to their market practices. Some people objected to their monopolistic market positions, especially western farmers, who often faced these combinations directly as buyers or as shippers of their produce. Others decried their political power and the vicious tactics used by the trusts to eliminate their independent rivals. In the late 1880s state laws tried to deal with these industrial giants. They did not work. A trust or monopolistic combine, threatened in one state, could simply move its legal residence across the state line. The Sherman Act, passed by Congress in 1890, finally seemed to answer the demands of the "antitrust movement." Its heart lies in two short sections, the original text of which can be quoted in full:

> Sec. 1. Every contract, combination in the form of trust or otherwise, or conspiracy, in restraint of trade or commerce among the several States, or with foreign nations, is hereby declared to be illegal. Every person who shall make any such contract or engage in any such combination or conspiracy, shall be deemed guilty of a misdemeanor, and, on conviction thereof, shall be punished by fine not exceeding five thousand dollars, or by imprisonment not exceeding one year, or by both said punishments, in the discretion of the court.
>
> Sec. 2. Every person who shall monopolize, or attempt to monopolize, or combine or conspire with any other person or persons, to monopolize any part of the trade or commerce among the several States, or with foreign nations, shall be deemed guilty of a misdemeanor, and, on conviction thereof, shall be punished by fine not exceeding five thousand dollars, or by imprisonment not exceeding one year, or by both said punishments, in the discretion of the court.

Now, what do these words mean as restraints on monopoly power? The first section, clearly enough, attacks the *act* of combining or conspiring to restrain trade. Taken at its word, "every" formal arrangement among firms aimed at curbing independent actions in the market seems to become illegal. This section restricts market conduct, especially those means of coordinating sellers in the market which use formal agreements to reduce the independence of their actions. The second section of the Sherman Act turns to situations of monopoly. Thus it would seem to enjoin certain market structures, with seller concentration so high that we could call it monopoly. Or does it? The words of the statute speak not of "monopoly"—the state of market structure—but of "monopolizing"—the act of creating a high level of seller concentration. What about a monopoly, in existence, but not the manifest work of some person or persons currently acting to monopolize? Does Section 2, then, outlaw a class of market structures, or does it simply repeat the ban laid down by Section 1 against certain classes of market conduct? The Sherman Act, like other antitrust statutes, is not self-enforcing. What its words mean in practice depends on what sense the federal courts make of them, for enforcement comes through the United States Attorney General bringing charges against persons for violating the law. When such persons deny their guilt, the issue goes before the courts to determine the validity of the charges. Thus the courts have wide latitude in interpreting the meaning of the key sections of the Sherman Act. But before we see what the courts have actually made of it, let us summarize the later pieces of legislation that round out the present set of antitrust statutes.

### Clayton and Federal Trade Commission Acts of 1914

The first two decades of experience with the Sherman Act hardly satisfied its original supporters. By 1914 strong pressure had built up in support of two sorts of extension of the antitrust laws beyond what the Sherman Act contained: (1) outlawing specific business practices that seemed to restrain trade; and (2) establishing a specialized administrative agency to lay down rules marking out "good" and "bad" patterns of business conduct. The Clayton and Federal Trade Commission Acts, passed in that year, wrote these two reforms respectively into law.

The Federal Trade Commission Act established the commission of that name with rather wide powers to investigate "the organization, business conduct, practices, and management" of companies engaging in interstate commerce. The statute also gave the commission a new piece of antitrust legislation to enforce, in the flat statement that "Unfair methods of competition in commerce are hereby declared unlawful." It remained for the commission to decide what is "unfair." In making such determinations, the commission could issue "cease and desist orders." After an amendment to the legislation in 1938, these orders became binding after 60 days unless appealed to the courts. On the face of it, an economist is hard put to figure out what the key word "unfair" adds to the ban on actions in restraint of trade contained in the Sherman Act. And the Federal Trade Commission indeed found no distinctive role for its enforcement activities until much later, when the Wheeler-Lea Act of 1938 added "unfair or deceptive acts or practices in commerce" to the actions that the commission could seek to block. Thereupon, the commission set forth in pursuit of deceptive advertising practices.

The Clayton Act attacked a series of business policies insofar as they would "substantially lessen competition or tend to create a monopoly." It forbade mergers that were undesirable by this test. The antimerger provision lay dormant for many years because its language restricted only mergers brought about by one particular legal process. This loophole was closed in 1950 by the Celler-Kefauver Act, and the antimerger provision has since taken on great importance. It now restricts not only "horizontal" mergers between competitors but also acquisitions of companies in any line of commerce where the effect might be to lessen competition. The Clayton Act also limits price discrimination and forbids certain practices of the seller that tend to limit the access of his buyers to other sellers.

## ANTITRUST AND MARKET STRUCTURE

Each piece of antitrust legislation has a complex and varied history of enforcement. Although violations of some antitrust provisions can be taken to court by private parties who feel that they have been harmed, the main burden of enforcement lies with agencies of the federal government—the Justice Department and the Federal Trade Commission. The government's fervor for enforcing the laws has varied greatly over the years. It hit bottom from 1893 to 1895 when Richard Olney, the U.S. Attorney General, made it plain that he thought the Sherman Act was effectively without legal force. Antitrust enforcement probably reached its peak of activity in the late 1930s under Assistant Attorney General Thurman Arnold, when wags began to refer to the 1890 legislation as the "Thurman Act." Another reason for the checkered history of antitrust enforcement lies in the attitude of the judges in the federal courts, particularly the Supreme Court justices, whose decision in cases that they hear on appeal place the flesh of interpretation on the bones of the statutes passed by Congress. The Court often seeks to maintain the attitude that its decisions, decade by decade, century by century, form a consistent and unchanging pattern. In fact, the judicial mind has undergone some marked changes over the years in interpreting the major antitrust statutes. Referring to a few key cases, let us see what sense the courts have made of the antitrust provisions affecting market structure.

### Monopoly

We saw that the words of Section 2 of the Sherman Act permit very different interpretations. Is it a crime to *have* a monopoly, to *seek* a monopoly, or to *seek and get* a monopoly? Not until 1911 did the Supreme Court decide cases concerning two giant trusts of the time—Standard Oil and American Tobacco. These two firms came close to monopolizing two major United States industries. About 91 percent of the refining industry was under direct or indirect control of Standard Oil, and the Tobacco Trust held between three-fourths and nine-tenths of the market for every tobacco product except cigars. Furthermore, both firms had lurid reputations for using questionable tactics to force small rivals to abandon the market or sell out to the trusts. If these firms were not guilty of monopolizing, then clearly Section 2 of the Sherman Act had no practical effect.

The Supreme Court indeed found both firms guilty under both Sections 1 and 2 and ordered their dissolution into several independent firms.[1] But its reasoning took a very particular view about the meaning of the Sherman Act. When Congress outlawed "every...combination...in restraint of trade" (Section 1), did it really mean to impose a sweeping ban? Or did it intend implicitly to bar only "unreasonable" restraints of trade, those that substantially infringed on the public welfare? The Supreme Court in 1911 took the latter view, enunciating the famous "rule of reason" in interpreting the Sherman Act. Standard Oil and American Tobacco were guilty because they had restrained trade *unreasonably*, not just because they had restrained trade. Furthermore, the decisions emphasized, not the high levels of seller concentration that prevailed, but rather the vicious practices that had been used to dispatch smaller competitors. What if a firm held a near-monopoly of its market, but had won it without making any specific predatory attacks on its rivals? Such an action, the decision implied, might not unreasonably restrain trade.

Later decisions quickly confirmed the narrow scope left by the "rule of reason" interpretation of violations of Section 2 of the Sherman Act. Eastman Kodak, United Shoe Machinery Corp., and International Harvester each held a near-monopoly of its industry. But in each case the courts found nothing offensive because the dominant firm had not visibly coerced or attacked what few rivals it had. The most famous of such cases, decided in 1920, involved United States Steel, then the nation's largest industrial firm.[2] Like the oil and tobacco giants, U.S. Steel was formed by combining a large number of formerly independent companies into an enterprise that originally held 60 percent of the nation's iron and steel capacity. After its formation, however, U.S. Steel refrained from coercing its remaining rivals. Indeed, it even "held an umbrella" over their profits by working to prevent price competition in the industry, and, perhaps because of this, its 60 percent market share slowly declined. Viewing Big Steel in 1920, the Supreme Court found it not in violation of the Sherman Act. The evidence did not show that it had mistreated its competitors or, during the decade of 1911 to 1920, had conspired to fix prices. Furthermore, "the law does not make mere size an offense or the existence of unexerted power an offense." This brought the point into sharp relief. Only monopolizing, and not monopoly, constituted an offense.

This interpretation in regard to monopolies and near-monopolies in the American economy stood for two decades after the steel decision. The Sherman Act did not in those years restrict monopolistic market structures. "Mere size" could be an offense only if accompanied by certain nasty types of market conduct. But a major change came in 1945 with the final decision in a case charging that the Aluminum Company of America (Alcoa) had violated Section 2 of the Sherman Act

[1]*U.S.* v. *Standard Oil Co. of New Jersey*, 221 U.S. 1 (1911); *U.S.* v. *American Tobacco Co.*, 221 U.S. 106 (1911).
[2]*U.S.* v. *U.S. Steel Corp.*, 251 U.S. 417 (1920).

by monopolizing the manufacture of newly refined aluminum.[3] For the first time, the Court took the view that a high level of seller concentration itself could constitute a violation of Section 2. The 90 percent of United States virgin aluminum production that Alcoa controlled "is enough to constitute a monopoly; it is doubtful whether sixty or sixty-four percent would be enough; and certainly thirty-three percent is not." Whether or not this is the *right* standard for deciding what level of seller concentration violates Section 2 of the Sherman Act, the important fact remains that a standard centering on market structure replaced one that depended essentially on market conduct.

> The Court in the Alcoa decision did not skip over the fact that Section 2 contains the word "monopolize" and not the word "monopoly." However, it moved away from the older view, which saw an intent to monopolize only in overt attempts to weaken and destroy particular business rivals. The court found that Alcoa's monopoly was not "thrust upon it." Instead, by a series of normal, prudent, but not predatory business practices the firm had succeeded in discouraging or forestalling all would-be competitors. These included building capacity well ahead of demand. As we have seen, barriers to entry into an industry do not exist just because the going firms threaten to wage war against a newcomer. The Alcoa decision gave this view some legal standing, recognizing that a firm can gain and protect a monopoly position in ways more subtle than taking the bloody axe to its competitors.

The years just after World War II brought several other cases that moved the Sherman Act closer to the regulation of market structure. Section 2 proved able, for the first time, to deal with a small group of firms jointly dominating the market. In 1946 the three largest cigarette producers, which then controlled about five-sixths of the United States cigarette market, were convicted of violating the act. The evidence did not show that they had conspired to intimidate their rivals, or even that they had overtly conspired at all. Instead, it showed that the three had acted in closely parallel fashion *as if* they were taking full account of their influence on one another and on the market. In short, the concept of "monopolizing" was extended to cover an industry with high concentration and tacit, rather than open, collusion. This case supplies an important moral for any who propose extended use of the Sherman Act against such "close-knit" oligopolies. The U.S. government never secured any remedy from the courts to prevent further violations by the cigarette industry. Indeed, how could it? The "crime" essentially consisted of a few firms taking one another's presence into account. They could hardly stop doing this unless their number were increased considerably. And the cigarette case *did not* establish that domination of the market by three firms constitutes a monopoly and warrants breaking up the firms. Thus the case extended the coverage of the Sherman Act but failed to provide any remedy for the legal abuse that it identified.

The cigarette case left the implication that the close recognition of mutual interdependence by oligopolists might be illegal, and yet it opened no avenue toward dealing with this situation. Some other cases that have followed in the wake

---

[3]*U.S.* v. *Aluminum Co. of America*, 148 F.2d 416 (1945).

of the Alcoa decision did take the logical step of recognizing that monopolistic market structures could stem from market conduct designed to create and sustain them. The Alcoa case hinted at this possibility by asserting that a company acting in a way that discourages the entry of rivals could hardly be unconscious of the outcome of its deeds. In a 1953 case the United Shoe Machinery Co. was found guilty of monopolizing the shoe-machinery industry, in large part because its record of conduct was clearly designed to forestall competition.[4] Divestiture was not a feasible remedy in this case, so the court instead enjoined an extensive array of practices that the company had used to place entrants and small competitors at a disadvantage. The United Shoe Machinery decision is noteworthy in two ways for its use of economic analysis: (1) its appreciation of the ability of market behavior to alter market structure by erecting entry barriers, and (2) its recognition that poor allocative efficiency is not likely to stem from high seller concentration by itself but from high concentration supported by barriers to entry.

Recent years have brought no more landmark decisions by the Supreme Court. Two important cases were terminated short of court decisions. A case against AT&T, charging monopolization of telephone equipment and long-distance telephone service, was ended by a consent decree in 1982. That decree had important consequences for increasing competition in these markets, but it left no tracks on the prevailing legal standards. A major case against IBM for monopolizing the computer industry was dropped by the government short of a decision at about the same time. (We will consider the IBM case in a moment.)

In the meantime, lower courts have decided various cases in ways that clearly suggest reversion from the standard represented by Alcoa and United Shoe Machinery back toward the rule of reason. In a private suit brought by Telex Corporation against IBM, the circuit court declined to see as conducive to entry barriers various business policies with that distinct flavor.[5] And in another private suit brought by Berkey Photo against Eastman Kodak Co., the circuit court was similarly disinclined to see barrier-building conduct, and it gave weight to the lack of evidence of predatory intent.[6] Neither decision was further considered by the Supreme Court, leaving room to surmise that the high court would not have disagreed with them. Thus, it is a fair bet that the standard on monopoly cases has retreated from Alcoa and United Shoe Machinery.

### Mergers

The antitrust laws for many years could be used to halt only those industrial mergers big enough to violate the Sherman Act's test of monopolization. Only in the late 1950s did court decisions confirm that the amended legislation had become an effective barrier to mergers that "tend to create a monopoly." The antitrust

---

[4]*U.S.* v. *United Shoe Machinery Corp.*, 110 F.Supp. 295 (1953).
[5]*Telex Corporation* v. *IBM Corporation*, 510 F.2d 894 (1975).
[6]*Berkey Photo Inc.* v. *Eastman Kodak Co.*, 603 F.2d 263 (1979).

officials have since been able to win a very high proportion of the cases they brought, so that mergers may be illegal between firms that control a very small percentage of business in a narrowly defined market. The "low water mark" was a case that blocked a merger between two grocery chains in Los Angeles that accounted for only 7.5 percent of grocery sales there.[7] Another case stopped a merger between two shoe companies accounting together for 4.5 percent of United States production.[8] The Court's attitude has been that mergers between competitors carry a tendency toward monopoly that should be nipped in the bud. Given the difficulty of deconcentrating an industry once it becomes concentrated, one can perhaps understand this low tolerance for increases.[9] It is disappointing, though, that these merger cases paid so little attention to the presence or absence of entry barriers, which determine whether the removal of one small competitor by merger is likely to have any significant effect on market performance.

During the 1970s, however, the courts and the Federal Trade Commission came to give more weight to these factors. The Federal Trade Commission, for example, let stand an acquisition in the frozen pizza market of a firm with a 1.7 percent market share by one holding 15.4 percent. The Commission held that entry barriers were low and that the acquired firm had no substantial competitive significance for the industry's leaders.[10] During the 1980s the government looked the other way while large mergers occurred in petroleum and other industries.

Antitrust law restricts not only horizontal mergers between competitors but also vertical mergers between customer and supplier, and diversified (or conglomerate) mergers between unrelated firms. Court decisions have not carefully articulated a basis for determining when these mergers tend to lessen competition or create a monopoly. Vertical mergers have been found objectionable because (for example) the seller who acquires his customer "forecloses" other sellers from seeking the customer's business; "substantial foreclosure" is a basis for rejecting a vertical merger. The difficulty with this concept as an economic standard is that foreclosure means that transactions between the formerly independent parties now pass through a single administrative apparatus; foreclosure defines the event and does nothing to indicate its significance. As we saw in Chapter 3, vertical integration can raise entry barriers, but it can also bring efficiency. A flat prohibition does not seem appropriate.

Conglomerate mergers have been rejected on the "deep pocket" hypothesis— the idea that a large, diversified company would acquire another company, smaller in total size but a leader in its market, and use its resources to drive out the small

[7]*U.S.* v. *Von's Grocery Co. et al.*, 384 U.S. 270 (1966).

[8]*Brown Shoe Co.* v. *U.S.*, 370 U.S. 294 (1962). For an analysis of this case, which also had aspects of vertical integration and monopoly in shoe retailing, see John L. Peterman, "The Brown Shoe Case," *Journal of Law and Economics*, Vol. XVIII (April 1975), pp. 81–147.

[9]Another complicating fact is that, although the government can block nearly any merger, it cannot always restore the acquired firm to independent viability. See Kenneth Elzinga, "The Antimerger Law: Pyrrhic Victories?" *Journal of Law and Economics*, Vol. XII (April 1969), pp. 43–78. Legislation in 1976 required merging companies to give the antitrust officials some advance notice, making it somewhat easier to stay a merger that might prove both illegal and irreversible after the event.

[10]*In the Matter of the Pillsbury Company et al.*, 93 FTC 966 (1979).

company's competitors. Economic analysis supplies one basis for a tough line on conglomerate mergers. If larger firms are discouraged from making diversified acquisitions, they might enter new industries by building a new plant, or acquiring a small and struggling competitor rather than a market leader, and the competitive discipline of the threat of entry would be increased. On the other hand, we should not discourage diversified mergers more than necessary, because they are a part of the "market for corporate control." That is, we want entrepreneurs to have the option of selling out their company when they retire, or when they think their talents are better used in another business.

Although past court decisions have supported stringent restraints on vertical and conglomerate mergers, we should stress that for two decades the antitrust authorities have shown little inclination to enforce them. In fact, firms making vertical and conglomerate mergers nowadays have little fear that the antitrust whistle will be blown.

## ANTITRUST LAWS AND MARKET CONDUCT

The antitrust laws also deal with several aspects of business conduct. They restrict joint actions by firms that aim to monopolize the market and also policies of individual firms that can impair competition or raise entry barriers.

### Combinations in Restraint of Trade

Enforcement of the Sherman Act against sellers who make collusive agreements has proved much simpler than against firms with near-monopoly power. Here the words of Section 1, "every contract, combination, or conspiracy," have been taken at their face value. All types of agreements to restrain trade have been outlawed—agreements to fix or maintain prices, to limit output or productive capacity, to share markets, to share profits through a common sales agency, and so forth. Furthermore, no "rule of reason" has entered into the decisions condemning formal conspiracies in restraint of trade. The courts have never asked whether such agreements aimed at reasonable objectives, or achieved reasonable results. In legal parlance such restraints of trade have always been held illegal *per se*. Punishments for firms found guilty of entering into these agreements have been of one or both of two kinds. Criminal penalties have taken the form of relatively insignificant fines. So-called civil remedies, aimed at preventing the abuse from recurring, have taken the more decisive form of enjoining any further use of the agreements in question.

> Despite the number of convictions for price-fixing, some economists have wondered whether enjoining them really brings much improvement in performance. If market structure remains as it was, can the prosecution of a price-fixing arrangement bring a permanent increase in competition? The historical evidence does suggest that most structural remedies—dissolutions of monopoly firms—have accomplished their objective. After the 1911 decision, for example, the Standard Oil trust was dissolved into a number of component companies, each marketing a different section of the country.

The firms stuck to their own territories for many years, but they eventually began competing on each other's turf, bringing more market rivalry to gasoline retailing. Can we equally promote competition in the long run by making effective collusion more difficult? Whatever their long-run effects, prosecutions of price-fixing conspiracies evidently do some good in the short run. In 1961 the Federal Trade Commission brought a complaint against a conspiracy among bakers and food chains to fix the price of bread in the State of Washington. The conspirators apparently managed to nudge the Seattle retail price upward about 15 percent over the United States average at the time the appellate court found against the bakers. About a month later, Seattle bread prices started to slip, then dropped sharply to levels at or below the nationwide average.[11]

The only type of combination among competing firms that is subject to a test of reasonableness (rather than being outright illegal) is the trade association. Some trade associations have served as vehicles for price-fixing, in which case they become clearly illegal. Their principal function, however, is to gather information and disseminate it to their members. Providing information on overall trends in the market clearly can improve performance by reducing the errors in managers' guesses about the future. Some kinds of information supplied by trade associations, however, can restrict competition by helping members to fix prices or to detect violations of collusive agreements by other sellers. Because some trade-association practices are desirable, public policy should restrict only those trade associations whose actions work to restrain trade to an unreasonable degree. The courts have come around to just about this view of the trade association under Section 1 of the Sherman Act.

Until the Alcoa decision (1945) displaced the 1911 "rule of reason" for cases involving monopoly, a strange contrast prevailed between the intensity of enforcement against monopolies and that against conspiracies in restraint of trade. It was justly called a "double standard." Agreements among firms were ruled out by the courts, regularly and without regard to their reasonableness. But if these conspiring firms had merged instead, accomplishing the same economic results more easily as a single-firm monopoly than through agreements among independent sellers, they would probably have gotten off under the rule of reason. Indeed, some people fear that the Sherman Act *promoted* higher seller concentration during these years because of its stiffer treatment of the kind of conspiracies that existed in industries with only moderately high concentration. With Alcoa's test for monopolization now somewhat eclipsed, the double standard may be with us once again.

### Business Practices

If the Sherman Act is ambivalent about whether *having* a monopoly is illegal, it unquestionably restricts predatory behavior designed to *get* a monopoly. The outcomes of the old Standard Oil and American Tobacco cases were largely

---

[11]Russell C. Parker, "The Baking Industry," *Antitrust Law and Economics Review*, Vol. II (Summer 1969), pp. 111–122.

determined by the evidence that the accused firms had sought to destroy their competitors. A company cannot charge a lower price in one location than in another if the court concludes that its intent was to drive a local competitor out of business.

But the antitrust laws also restrict some conduct that is more subtle in its intended effects. Section 3 of the Clayton Act forbids a seller to require buyers of its line of goods to refrain from purchasing goods from its rivals, where the policy lessens competition or tends to create a monopoly. This clause restricts two methods of excluding competitors. It blocks *tying arrangements*, whereby a seller gives the buyer access to one line of the seller's goods only if the buyer takes others as well. A tying arrangement exists, for instance, when a firm selling stapling machines requires that its stapling-machine customers purchase their staples from it as well. This prohibition has been enforced very strictly, although the court decisions do not explain very clearly why tying occurs or what its effects are. Why should our maker of stapling machines restrict its customers' purchases to its own staples? If it charges more than the market price for staples, customers are less willing to pay for its stapling machines and will shift their demands toward competing suppliers. If the seller monopolizes stapling machines, why does it not simply charge the price for them that maximizes monopoly profits? Most tying arrangements we observe do involve some monopoly power in the tying good—the stapling machine, in our example. And tying does contribute to monopoly profits, but in a special way. The stapling machine generally must be sold at the same price to all buyers—those who will use it a great deal (and value it highly) as well as those who use it only occasionally (finding it just worth its cost). By raising the price of staples and tying the machine to their use, the seller has a way to capture some of the "surplus" from customers who use the machine a lot and therefore require many staples. This policy is a form of price discrimination that tends to reduce economic welfare, and so its prevention is probably desirable.

Somewhat similar to tying arrangements are *exclusive-dealing arrangements*, whereby a seller gives the buyer access to his line of goods only if the buyer agrees to take no goods from any of the seller's rivals. For instance, a gasoline refiner might require that its franchised service stations handle only its gasoline, and its own line of tires, batteries, and accessories as well. The motive of the manufacturer using exclusive dealing is to further the public image of its product by controlling the circumstances under which it is sold and the service provided with it (important in the case of durable goods). The main economic argument against exclusive dealing arrangements lies in their effect on entry barriers into the manufacturing activity. If there are natural limits on the number of retail outlets suitable to handle a product, and existing ones are tied down by exclusive-dealing contracts, the new manufacturer faces the additional burden of developing new retail outlets. This burden could create a substantial absolute capital cost barrier to entry. The courts have seen the problem in this fashion and have restricted exclusive dealing when used in parallel by dominant sellers, placing newcomers or fringe sellers at a disadvantage.

We have already noted that price discrimination is outlawed where it is intended to drive out a competitor, or where it takes the form of a tying arrangement. Further restrictions were placed on it by the Robinson-Patman Act of 1936, which was explicitly intended to help small business. The act was not aimed at price discrimination in general, but at preventing price discrimination in favor of the large buyers (the chain store) or even at forcing discrimination against large buyers. Its main provision forbids a seller "to discriminate in price between different purchasers of commodities of like grade and quality" under certain conditions. The seller may not discriminate when the result "may be substantially to lessen competition or tend to create a monopoly in any line of commerce" or to "injure, destroy, or prevent competition with any person who either grants or knowingly receives the benefits of such discrimination." Discrimination becomes illegal when it harms competitors, as well as when it harms competition. The two are not the same thing. The less competition there is, the happier competitors are. A healthy process of competition destroys inefficient competitors without seriously raising the level of concentration in the market.

To analyze the main provisions of the Robinson-Patman Act, we note that its enforcement machinery starts to grind when the same good or service is observed to be sold to different parties at different prices. The accused seller might plead various defenses:

1. *The buyers are not in the same market*, so that a discount to one does not harm the other. A maker of spark plugs can sell them much more cheaply to an auto company than to the general public without violating the law. It is still price discrimination, but the Robinson-Patman Act is concerned only with discrimination between directly competing buyers.

2. *The accused seller is merely meeting offers made by his competitors.* The law permits sporadic price discrimination to meet the competition, but a seller cannot justify sustained or systematic price discrimination on this basis. Nor can the seller justify having cut the price for selected buyers in order to get new business.

3. *The price differences actually reflect cost differences*, in which case there is no price discrimination. One might expect sellers to make frequent use of this defense because many businesses surely have some fixed costs of filling an order that do not increase much with the order's size, and so average out less for big orders. But a cost defense is difficult to sustain before the Federal Trade Commission, and it is not often used.

The effects of the Robinson-Patman Act on market performance have been mixed at best. It eliminated many discounts to large buyers that reflected only bargaining power and not true cost savings. It was able to stop chain stores that were trying to destroy local competitors. Both of these results are favorable. On the other hand, it tended to reduce the vigor of price competition. In loose-knit oligopolies where price is pushed somewhat above marginal cost, price rivalry often does not come about through changes in list prices but via sporadic, unsystematic discounts (or premiums) that spread through the market until they burst forth as cuts (or increases) in list prices. These sporadic price differences amount to temporary price discrimination. With the Robinson-Patman Act threatening their legality, sellers may play it safe and hold the line on prices. Price flexibility in some industries may have been reduced.[12] In the 1960s antitrust officials became convinced of these negative features of the Robinson-Patman Act and greatly reduced their efforts to enforce it.

## ANTITRUST: ISSUES ON THE FRONTIER

The historical evolution of antitrust policy provides essential background for understanding the legal standards that now prevail and the influence they have wielded on the structure and behavior of the economy. But we also need some feeling for the issues recently active. Some emerge from major antitrust cases or investigations. Others turn up in debates on antitrust policy among economists and others.

### Some Strategic Cases

Every market shows its own distinctive combination of structure and behavior, and so each antitrust case raises new issues about an industry's constellation of market structure and conduct and the market performance that it yields. One such case dealt with IBM's alleged monopolization of the market for general-purpose electronic computer systems. Brought by the Justice Department in 1969, the case was dropped by the government in 1982 before a court decision was reached. The legal sparring over the case was largely concerned with the definition of the market: IBM's share could be three-fourths or one-third, depending on whether the market was large, general-purpose systems or a chain of substitutes running all the way to hand-held calculators. However, the more interesting issue in the case was the practices that IBM employed at certain times to place its competitors at a disadvantage and raise barriers to entry. IBM no doubt reached its initial dominant position through innovative performance, recognizing the potential for computer applications to business problems and developing the software and support services needed to bring this unfamiliar technology into widespread business use. That innovative lead was maintained, however, by some dubious practices.[13] IBM bundled its services together, encouraging its customers to lease rather than buy their machines and rolling the provision of software and servicing into the package. The practice of leasing tended to raise the capital-cost entry barriers for entrants, and the tying of software and servicing discouraged the development of specialist firms that might later have expanded to become broad-based competitors. Similarly, IBM employed various policies to discourage independent producers of peripheral equipment that was "plug compatible" with IBM mainframe computers. When rivals in the mainframe-computer market offered models with more computing power for

---

[12]For a classic study of the Robinson-Patman Act, see Corwin D. Edwards, *The Price Discrimination Law: A Review of Experience* (Washington, DC: Brookings Institution, 1959), especially Chap. 19.

[13]See Gerald W. Brock, *The U.S. Computer Industry: A Study of Market Power* (Cambridge, MA: Ballinger, 1975).

the price than IBM's, buyers were deterred from placing orders by IBM's announcement that it was bringing out a better model still—even though IBM then underwent a protracted pregnancy before the new model emerged.

These practices posed for antitrust policy the problem of drawing the line between vigorous competition and use of a dominant position to weaken competitors and raise entry barriers. But the IBM case raised another dilemma. Competition in the industry increased greatly over the decade-plus that it was in the works. IBM might well have flunked the Alcoa test in 1969 yet have been innocent on the facts of the early 1980s. The hopes for effective antitrust enforcement are certainly impaired if an industry can proceed through a major phase of its evolution while our court system is resolving a case.

A case brought by the Federal Trade Commission against the leading producers of ready-to-eat breakfast cereals also touched on entry deterrence. The three leading producers jointly commanded 81 percent of the market. None of their individual shares approached the Alcoa threshold of 60 to 64 percent, although a novel legal feature of the FTC's case was its attempt to make the combined 81 percent share stand as evidence of shared monopoly, in light of the extensive parallelism of the companies' market behavior. In that respect, the breakfast-cereal case harks back to American Tobacco (the 1946 case). Its economic interest lies in the companies' behavior and some of the performance it produced. The high level of concentration apparently cannot be explained at all by scale economies in production. Advertising levels have been very high (16 percent of sales), and so have profits. In contrast to many lines of grocery-store products, the cereal makers have faced little competition from private-label brands sponsored by supermarket chains, perhaps because they themselves have been unwilling to produce for private labels. The industry has bestirred much discussion of "brand proliferation" as the six leading firms' brands expanded from 27 in 1950 to 71 in 1971. Was this expansion to fill niches in the market that entrants might otherwise occupy, or were the cereal-makers just offering different breakfasts for different tastes?[14] The FTC dismissed this case.

A third case, decided in 1977,[15] addressed the relations between a manufacturing firm and the distributors of its product. The issue was whether the manufacturer should be allowed to limit the competition among its own retail distributors in offering the product to final buyers. Why should such competition be other than a good thing? Also, why should the manufacturer not want the distributors to compete vigorously? If they did, they would work on the thinnest possible margin between wholesale and retail price and thus allow the manufacturer the maximum profit. In 1977 the Supreme Court found itself facing these questions. It recognized that the manufacturer might have valid reasons for limiting competition among its distributors, and these reasons might reflect a social interest as well. Product differentiation is the key. The manufacturer of a complex branded product—TV

[14]Richard Schmalensee, "Entry Deterrence in the Ready-to-Eat Breakfast Cereal Industry," *Bell Journal of Economics*, Vol. IX (Autumn 1978), pp. 305–327.

[15]*Continental T.V., Inc. et al.*, v. *GTE Sylvania, Inc.*, 433 U.S. 36 (1977).

sets, in this case—depends on retail dealers to provide information and assistance to potential buyers, to offer prompt and reliable after-sales service, and to build up goodwill for the manufacturer in other ways. The manufacturer gets benefits from the dealer's earnest efforts beyond the profits that the dealer collects. The manufacturer's problem, then, is how to motivate the dealer to provide enough of them. The best way to align the dealer's interests with the manufacturer's own may be to limit "intrabrand competition" at retail, fattening the dealer's margins enough to encourage the appropriate effort.[16] If this maker's TV sets compete with enough other TV sets on the market, then the manufacturer's restriction of intrabrand competition is not automatically a bad thing. Indeed, the Supreme Court held that it might be legal or illegal, depending on the facts of the case. Before 1977 it had been illegal *per se* to restrict dealers to territories in which they did not compete with one another.

### General Issues

Other frontier issues in antitrust policy lie beyond the particular cases. One of them concerns an enforcement mechanism: the private antitrust suit. Under the Sherman Act, a party injured by a firm violating the act can bring a private suit in the courts. The plaintiff who wins stands to collect three times the amount of the damages that the court estimates were suffered. On first thought, private antitrust suits might seem merely a desirable supplement to enforcement by the Justice Department and Federal Trade Commission. Certainly the penalties levied by some private cases have been large enough to make the potential antitrust violator stay on the path of virtue.

However, economists sympathetic with the general goals of antitrust policy have entertained some doubts about these private suits. First, they are often settled out of court and out of the reach of public policy. The settlements may involve not just cash changing hands but also policy commitments made by the accused to the plaintiff. About one-third of these suits seem to be brought against firms by their direct competitors. Can one doubt that these settlements sometimes involve a promise not to compete so vigorously? Second, the trebling of damages may have its disadvantages, however much it deters antitrust violations. With such big prizes being handed out, plaintiffs have an incentive to bring suits with little substantive merit, on the chance that their lucky number might come up. Or they might lie low and tolerate an antitrust violation, rather than screaming promptly for help, in order to run up the damages to be trebled. So private enforcement has its drawbacks.

Another general issue, always with us in one form or another, is the charge that antitrust policy somehow discourages cooperative efforts by American business that might bring great benefits to the country. Usually this position germinates from someone's belief in endless economies of scale or a powerful affinity between

---

[16]The manufacturer may be unable to write or enforce a contract specifying the services that the distributor is to provide, so the next best option is to fatten the distributor's margin and make it profitable for the distributor to offer more blandishments to the customer.

monopoly and innovation; neither belief, we have seen, accords well with the empirical evidence. Recently, however, this policy position has taken its cue from the relatively greater success of other industrial countries (notably Japan) and their leading firms, and the alleged need of U.S. business to stand up to its foreign rivals. The issues here are numerous and complex. For example, one can ask whether the success of leading business enterprises in other industrial countries bears any relations to softer competition policies in force abroad. The answer, quite clearly, is that the catch-up with the United States is if anything associated with increasing competitiveness in their home markets and more vigorous competition policies than prevailed abroad, say, 30 years ago. One can also ask whether good market performance necessarily has anything to do with competing successfully on world markets. The connection is fairly remote: International economists remind us that no country can have a comparative advantage in selling everything to the rest of the world. The general public—first in Europe, now in the United States—is all too prone to treat international competition as a sporting event. Our "national champion" should be able to jump as high as their national champion, and if not, our government should give it a boost. Economic analysis offers little support for this line of thought.

The valid concern connecting competition policy with international rivalry is the one mentioned in Chapters 1 and 2. Markets for many goods are growing more international in scope. Either industry boundaries should be drawn more widely than the single nation, in those cases, or we should recognize the compelling influence of international competition on conduct and performance in the domestic market. This recognition does not mean that we repeal the antitrust laws, but it does affect the proper strategy of enforcement.

## EXEMPTIONS FROM COMPETITION: THE PATENT SYSTEM

Despite the hallowed tradition of antitrust, America's laws exempt a number of sectors from legally enforced competition—agricultural cooperatives, labor unions, exporters' associations, and so on. Some exemptions have no obvious economic justifications, and so they do not raise problems about competition as a spur to effective performance. We shall examine, however, one exemption that does rest on an economic rationale—the patent system. A patent is a grant of a 17-year monopoly to an inventor, giving the patent-holder the right to exclude all others from duplicating the innovation for use or sale. By offering the inventor the promise of a monopoly over the exploitation of an invention for a fixed period of time, patents seek to encourage more inventive activity.

In the middle of the nineteenth century, the high tide of laissez-faire philosophy bred a school of thought opposed to the use of patents. A liberal sentiment that had fought against other types of government-sponsored restrictions on commercial freedom was not about to accept patents without question just because they claimed a justification for their monopoly privileges. However, this view lost out. Most countries continue to reward inventors, although many restrict patent monopolies to their own citizens and deny or limit them to foreign inventors.

The patent laws were originally directed toward independent inventors working independently in woodsheds or small shops. They were designed to repay them for their personal risk and expense. In contemporary America, however, the inventor has become the hired hand of the corporation. Now, at least 60 percent of all patents issued in the United States go promptly into the hands of corporations. This change in the process of invention has inevitably affected the role and function of the patent system, and we need to examine its place in a framework of corporate research and development to see if its grant of monopoly is still warranted. An appraisal of the patent system logically turns on the answers to these questions: (1) Without the patent system, would we get too few resources put into the quest for innovations? (2) Are there important incidental costs of the patent system?

The case for granting a patent to an inventor rests on the nature of the patented innovation as an idea. Making and selling ideas is a business unlike making and selling leather belts. Shoplifters apart, the beltmaker has no trouble getting payment from users of belts; the customer simply must pay before taking possession. Once the creator of ideas sells the inspiration to a customer, however, the cash compensation in the inventor's hand may be the last that is received. That is because the customer can resell the idea at no cost—the first customer still has use of it after reselling it to the second. The producer of intangible ideas gains no automatic property right in the output. The patent seeks to convey that property right—a monopoly that wards off all competitors, though only for a limited period of time. Without such protection the producer of ideas could not capture their value to the public, and would therefore produce too few—just like the beltmaker who cannot deter shoplifters.

Businesses that produce or develop new ideas are not without other ways to protect them. New production technology that lowers costs, for instance, can be kept secret from the firm's competitor—unless, of course, an employee who is in on the secret gets hired away. It has been said that businesses keep secret what innovations they can, and patent those which they cannot. Because securing a patent requires disclosing to the public what has been discovered, firms sometimes have reasons for preferring to do without it. Another protection to the innovating firm is simply its lead time over its rivals. Most of the innovative profits from fast-changing technologies must be captured before competitors can tool up to copy them, in which case patent protection may play a minor role.

We therefore need empirical evidence to tell us the importance of patents. Do large firms find them necessary in order to protect the substantial investments they make in perfecting an innovation and bringing it to market? Some manufacturers feel that patents are their lifeblood, and that their innovative activities would become unprofitable and would have to be dropped without them. Others indicate that patents make little difference in their search for, and introduction of, new products. Industries such as electronics, chemicals, and drugs make heavy use of patents; manufacturers of automobiles, paper, rubber, and heavy and light machinery do not.

The stimulus for innovation provided by the patent system depends partly on the market structure surrounding the innovator. Consider the firm that makes an important improvement in its product or production process. Patent protection is more important to the pure competitor than to the monopolist. First, because the monopoly has no rivals, it has no immediate imitators to compete away the profits of the innovation. The innovating firm in a purely competitive industry runs a high risk that, without patent protection, its brainstorm will be copied by rivals before the development costs can be recovered. Second, the innovator in a purely competitive industry has more to gain from a patented cost-reducing innovation than would a monopolist in the same setting, simply because the competitive industry produces a larger output. Therefore, more units of the competitive output stand ready to pay for the benefits of lower production costs. Empirical evidence confirms that patents are more important to small firms.[17]

Does the patent system impose social costs that weigh against its desirable encouragement to innovation? It gives the successful innovating firm a crack at whatever monopoly profit it can grab, and that monopoly has the same economic cost as other monopolies. Furthermore, the monopoly based on an initial patent can sometimes be augmented by entry barriers stemming from other sources, to make the resulting market power long-lasting. One authority listed aluminum, shoe machinery, plate glass, photographic equipment and supplies, ethyl fluid, braking systems, gypsum products, cigarettes, rayon, and metal containers as industries that grew highly concentrated on the basis of patents and then sustained their monopoly by other means. Furthermore, industries with high concentration have used their collective patent holdings as a basis for cross-licensing agreements among themselves that serve as a vehicle for joint monopolistic exploitation of their market. In this way the dominant firms of an industry can milk a combined number of patents for greater profits than could be obtained from each of the patents separately—at least until the antitrust officials catch up with them.

Another social cost arises because a patent, like any valuable monopoly position, induces others to expend resources in order to cut themselves in on the profits. When you discover a miracle-cure drug, for example, I will set to work trying to achieve the same therapeutic effect with a chemical different enough that I can also obtain a patent. If my cure works no better than yours, the resources I spent finding it are wasted from society's point of view.

As the outcome of a recent debate, antitrust authorities have made it clear that competing U.S. firms may enter into cooperative research projects without fear of being charged with collusion. Oddly enough, this policy grew out of public concern over whether U.S. industry could stand up effectively to its foreign competitors. Yet if the benefits (in more innovations or lower costs of innovating) exceed the small risk that colluding price-fixers will be decked out in lab coats, the presence of foreign competition is quite irrelevant.

[17]C. T. Taylor and Z. A. Silberston, *The Economic Impact of the Patent System* (Cambridge, England: Cambridge University Press, 1973); Richard C. Levin and others, "Appropriating the Returns from Industrial Research and Development," *Brookings Papers on Economic Activity*, Vol. 1987:3, pp. 783–820.

## SUMMARY

The antitrust laws seek to improve market performance by regulating market structure and conduct. The Sherman Act of 1890 forbade monopolizing and agreements in restraint of trade, and in 1914 the Clayton Act added restrictions on several kinds of market conduct. Mergers were effectively limited only in 1950.

The crime of monopolizing came to mean having a high market share that was secured by predatory attacks on competitors—that is, *unreasonable* restraint of trade. A near-monopoly not using predatory conduct was generally found within the law until 1945 (Alcoa). Subsequently, more attention was paid to conduct that builds entry barriers, but recently, policy has retreated toward the 1911 "rule of reason" standard. All types of mergers have come in for some limitation—horizontal, vertical, conglomerate. Horizontal mergers involving very small market shares can be blocked, but restrictions on horizontal mergers have recently been relaxed. The courts have at times placed stringent restrictions on vertical and conglomerate mergers, but these mergers may be beneficial, and antitrust authorities have made no significant effort to discourage them.

Prohibitions on predatory conduct and collusive price-fixing have been very strictly enforced. Also, individual sellers cannot preclude their buyers from purchasing from competing sellers, when the effect is to lessen competition. This prohibition restricts tying and exclusive dealing arrangements. Under the Robinson-Patman Act (1936), price discrimination is limited in ways designed to help small business.

The issues at the frontier of antitrust policy turn up both in particular cases and in general debates over policy. Important cases in recent years have dealt with competitive behavior likely to deter entry, both by the single dominant firm (IBM) and by highly concentrated sellers acting in parallel (the ready-to-eat cereal industry). Good and bad restrictive agreements between the manufacturer and his distributors have been defined more carefully. We have grown concerned about some side effects of private antitrust suits. And the United States has had trouble deciding how increased international competition should be related to competition policy.

Some activities and sectors of the economy are exempt from the antitrust laws. The exemption with the strongest economic rationale is probably the patent system, which gives the inventor a 17-year monopoly over the exploitation of an invention. Without the patent privilege, too few resources would be devoted to inventive activities because inventors could not keep other people from copying their ideas; also, the grant of a patent requires inventors to disclose their scientific discoveries, which otherwise would be kept secret. The patent privilege is particularly important to small firms, and provides a greater incentive for the pure competitor than for the established monopolist. But patents sometimes provide a basis for monopolies that persist long after the patent has expired, and they may encourage wasteful expenditures on imitation.

# Chapter 7

# Public Policy: Regulation and Public Enterprise

Is our best strategy for improving market performance the vigorous application of the antitrust laws? Or should we consider more drastic intervention into the market place? If market forces fail to set prices equal to marginal costs—the criterion for allocative efficiency—why not enact direct government regulation and order prices to be set that way? Or why not simply nationalize enterprises in malfunctioning industries and put them under the charge of civil servants (with degrees in economics)?

In this chapter we shall briefly consider the prospects of these more drastic forms of public policy intervention and our experience with them. We shall analyze them making use of the concepts of market structure, conduct, and performance already developed. In the past two decades some types of regulation have been relaxed or abandoned, while others have been added. Thus, we have plenty of "experiments" to observe.

## DIRECT REGULATION OF BUSINESS

In several important sectors of the American economy, especially public utilities and transportation, public policy has never tried to promote competition. Instead, it has resigned itself to monopolies serving local markets and has tried to devise a means of regulating the monopolies to secure reasonable economic performance. The local public utilities provide the clearest example of this market situation. Generally, the firms providing electric power, natural gas, telephone service, water, and bus transportation in a city hold monopoly positions that have been sanctioned by public authority and operate under detailed regulations governing their business practices. State and local regulators of other businesses subject entrants to some restriction through licensing or franchising, so the number of rivals is limited even if the markets are not run as monopolies. Sometimes the licensing is designed only to ensure that practitioners have proper qualifications for their jobs (as in medicine). In other cases (such as taxicabs), the government simply limits the resources in the industry to less than the market would provide.

Agencies of the federal government have wielded substantial regulatory powers over important industries, although many of these regulations have been relaxed or eliminated in the past decade. The Federal Energy Regulatory Commission has jurisdiction over the rates and services of interstate natural-gas pipelines having the status of common carriers and the field price of natural gas passing into these pipelines. It can also fix the wholesale rates for electrical energy transmitted interstate. Legislation passed in 1978 set in motion a complex decade-long relaxation of price controls over natural gas. The Federal Communications Commission regulates interstate telephone and telegraph rates and services. It also controls entry into radio and television broadcasting by parceling out the scarce supply of broadcasting channels; it holds some authority to influence the quality of broadcasting but has no control over prices. Cable television systems are no longer under its control, and the major increases in competition in long-distance telecommunications resulted from an antitrust case. The Interstate Commerce Commission, oldest of the federal regulatory commissions, long held the power to set the rates and services of railroads and highway common carrier trucking companies. Its authority over truckers' rates and services is now gone, and its control over railfreight rates is limited to settings in which the railroad possesses "market dominance." The Civil Aeronautics Board once wielded comprehensive authority over the routes and fares of interstate air carriers, but the agency is now out of business, and the airlines are subject only to safety regulation.

Any directory of regulatory agencies contains many more entries, but they have less to do with market structures. In the course of its responsibility for national monetary policy, the Federal Reserve Board regulates many aspects of the transactions of those commercial banks belonging to the Federal Reserve System. The Securities and Exchange Commission regulates securities dealers and exchanges in a way we might describe as insuring the "quality" of their services. It requires the disclosure of certain types of information about securities to investors and guards against a number of types of fraudulent dealings in the securities markets. Although the "old" regulators listed so far have relaxed most of their regulatory roles during the past decade, a new set of agencies has marched onto the scene to undertake "social" regulation—environmental pollution, safety of vehicles and other consumer products, occupational health and safety. Just as public policy became jaded with the old regulation, it grew enchanted with the new. We shall briefly note a few links between market structure and new regulation.

## Reasons for Regulation

Why did the old regulation come about? We can treat this as a historian's question about the events leading up to the political decision to place an activity under public regulation. Or we can treat it as an analytical question of why somebody's best interest should be served by putting the regulation into effect. The two approaches are, of course, not mutually exclusive: The analytical approach supplies hypotheses for the historian, and the historical evidence can confirm, reject, or modify the hypotheses.

*1. Correcting market failure.*    Traditionally, economists supposed that regulation arose to cope with noncompetitive market structures. The local public utilities supply the clearest examples. The production of most of their services involves scale economies that are large relative to their local markets. The utilities tend to have very high sunk costs, a condition that may make price competition work out badly unless many firms occupy the market. Demand is inelastic, so that a monopoly could wrest large profits away from the public. Competition would involve external diseconomies: Consider the annoyance of having to discover which of 30 telephone companies served your friend's house, or of finding one of 40 gas companies excavating the street each time a householder switches between suppliers. Therefore these markets are "natural monopolies."

The traditional explanation agrees nicely with the analysis of this book. Left alone, these market structures would exhibit poor allocative performance, poor technical efficiency, or both. We can hypothesize that the voters had the good sense to recognize that these industries were cases of "market failure" and bring them under regulation. Recently, however, other explanations have been advanced for regulation that draw upon models of political behavior in a more cynical way.

*2. Resolving political conflicts.*    Regulation might be imposed as a compromise solution to a political dispute. The farmers, let us suppose, feel that the railroads charge them too much to transport their grain to market. The railroads claim that they are earning only a reasonable and necessary profit. Both groups clamor for the government to protect their interests. The elected government (the president or the party in power) wants to find some way to keep both groups happy, because the government's own objective is to keep a majority of voters content with its policies so it can be reelected. There is no way the government can directly influence the price of grain transportation without offending at least one party. But regulation offers a possible solution. The government can appoint a regulatory commission to determine the right price, thereby removing the dispute from the political arena while appearing to deal fairly with it. And the regulatory commission can then provide its own solution, which might run as follows: The farmers want the low price, and the railroads want an acceptable level of profit. Both groups can be satisfied if the commission orders the low price for the farmers but at the same time permits (or requires) the railroads to charge higher prices to other shippers. If these other shippers are less sensitive to shipping costs than the farmers, or less well organized politically, this maneuver brings what we might call a new political equilibrium. Economically, other shippers are now "cross-subsidizing" the farmers by implicitly paying part of their transportation bills.[1]

*3. Providing political benefits.*    An even simpler political explanation holds that the government provides regulation to serve the interests of some group with the political power to demand it. An industry's members may recognize that regulation can be used to exclude new rivals and stifle competition among themselves. They decide that the potential profits make it worth the cost of lobbying to secure protective regulation. The general public are the losers, but nobody loses enough to expend the time and resources to oppose the industry's grab for benefits. This is the "capture" theory of regulation.[2] But the capture model in the form stated takes too narrow a view of political decisions. Consider the ambitious politician eager to appeal to a large mass of voters, who promises, if supported, to impose regulation to attain some generally popular goal, such as providing cheaper natural gas or cleaning up pollution. Many voters would enjoy benefits from such regulation that exceed what they expect (rightly or wrongly) would be the costs to them. The costs would either be concentrated on a minority of voters or are not anticipated by some of the majority. The politician gets the votes, and the industry is ordered to lower its natural-gas prices or invest in reducing its pollution. In short, political processes can generate either protective or punitive regulation, depending on how the expected benefits and costs are distributed and what opportunities arise for political entrepreneurs.[3]

Each of these models is "structural" in the sense of predicting the outcome of political decision making from a combination of economic elements of market structure and corresponding structural features of the political process. The market-failure hypothesis designates particular elements of market structure that make competition an ineffective process, and these structural features are clearly apparent in some regulated industries—local public utilities and railroads, for example. The cross-subsidy hypothesis implies that each regulated industry serves diverse groups of customers who have varying abilities to organize politically. That pattern has also been observed in the many geographically dispersed customers for transportation services, the distinguishable industrial, commercial, and residential customers for public utilities' services, and the like. The capture hypothesis predicts that regulation will appear where the consequence of monopolizing an industry is to provide highly concentrated wealth to the beneficiaries at a cost to the customers that is widely dispersed and small for the average buyer; in that case it will pay the industry to organize to secure protective regulation but will not pay members of the buying

[1]This model was advanced by John R. Baldwin, *The Regulatory Commission and the Public Corporation: The Canadian Air Transportation Industry* (Cambridge, MA: Ballinger, 1975); and Richard A. Posner, "Taxation by Regulation," *Bell Journal of Economics*, Vol. II (Spring 1971), pp. 22–50.

[2]George J. Stigler, "The Theory of Economic Regulation," *Bell Journal of Economics*, Vol. II (Spring 1971), pp. 3–21.

[3]James Q. Wilson, ed., *The Politics of Regulation* (New York: Basic Books, 1980), esp. Chap. 10.

public to organize to combat it. Occupational licensing by states and cities seems to provide many examples. The generalized model of political benefits and costs seems to explain much of the "new" social regulation as well as recent decisions to deregulate the airlines and the trucking industry despite the anguished cries of the regulated firms and their unionized employees.

## Economic Problems of Regulatory Decisions

For whatever reason businesses come to be regulated, there are important limitations on the process of economic regulation: what a regulatory agency is competent to decide and how a regulated business will react to its decisions. We must consider these problems before we can appraise the efficacy of regulation for improving market performance. To decide what price a regulated firm may charge, some regulatory agencies use a formula that can be described as allowing the firm to earn a "fair return on the fair value of its investment." This formula has been sanctioned by many decisions of the U.S. Supreme Court when regulatory decisions were appealed to it. The formula sounds consistent with allocative efficiency, as we defined it in Chapter 5. Firms in a purely competitive industry (producing under constant returns to scale) setting their outputs so that price equals marginal cost will just earn a normal rate of return on their capital; "normal" here refers to the market cost of capital in a competitive capital market. If a fair return on the fair value of a company's investment should roughly equal that normal return, is the company not being efficient?

Not necessarily. Assume that the regulatory commission indeed restricts a company to earn a profit rate on its capital that is less than the maximum monopoly profit it could earn, but more than the competitive opportunity cost of capital. The company no longer has an incentive to use only an efficient amount of capital. Suppose that in order to produce a given quantity of output, it builds a more capital-intensive plant than it would without regulation. The regulators let it set prices to earn a fair return on the inflated "fair value" of the plant, and the company has more dollars of profit than it otherwise would. Therefore we expect regulated companies to employ more capital-intensive technologies than an unregulated company would use to produce the same output. It could even be rational for regulated firms to let equipment suppliers overcharge them, because the fair value of their investment (their "rate base") goes up. The regulatory agency does not solve this problem by setting the fair rate of return equal to the market cost of capital. True, the utility can no longer get additional dollars of profit by inflating its capital stock. But by the same token it does not *lose* dollars of profit if it uses the wrong quantity, and there is no positive incentive for the efficient use of capital.

This bias toward capital intensity in rate-of-return regulation is known as the Averch-Johnson effect, for its principal publicists.[4] Some evidence concurs that regulated firms behave as the Averch-Johnson effect predicts. For example, the

---

[4]Harvey Averch and Leland Johnson, "Behavior of the Firm under Regulatory Constraint," *American Economic Review*, Vol. LII (December 1962), pp. 1052–1069.

efficient operation of an electric utility must take account of the fact that demand varies over the hours of the day and the seasons of the year. Because electricity must be produced at the same time it is consumed, the utility must keep its plant capacity large enough to meet its peak load, although it is underutilized the rest of the time. This waste can be reduced if the utility employs "peak load pricing," charging more at the time of peak usage and less at other times in order to flatten out the fluctuations in the quantities demanded. Electric utilities have been slow to adopt peak-load pricing, and the Averch-Johnson effect may supply the explanation. Peak-load pricing would reduce the size of the capital stock needed by the utility, and thereby reduce the profits allowed it under the fair-return formula.[5] Evidence of the Averch-Johnson effect does not by itself prove that the regulation is a bad thing, only that it has certain inefficiencies that must be set against its benefits. After all, the regulated firm exhibiting the Averch-Johnson effect will still be supplying a larger output than if it were an unregulated monopoly.

Another problem with firms' responses to regulatory decisions comes in industries like the airlines, where the regulated firms compete directly with one another. The Civil Aeronautics Board formerly had comprehensive authority to determine what fares the domestic airlines could charge, but it exerted little or no control over the nonprice dimensions of their competition. Consider what happened when the board set fares above the minimum attainable average (and marginal) cost of providing air transport. Unless the airlines colluded fully among themselves, each carrier faced the temptation to lure the extra passenger whose fare will exceed the marginal cost of serving him. The airline bought flossier aircraft, offered flights more frequently, gave the passenger more leg room, better meals, more personal pampering—all forms of nonprice competition that would increase demand and raise the carrier's market share if they were not matched by rival airlines. Of course, these moves also raised the carriers' average costs. Indeed, if the degree of mutual dependence recognized among the carriers was low enough, costs would adjust completely to the level of fares allowed by the board. That is, if the board decided that fares should be raised at a time when airlines' profits were normal, nonprice competitive responses by the carriers would raise costs until their temporarily inflated profits returned to the former level. Of course, the process would also work on the downside: A cut in fares would squeeze profits and induce the airlines to produce less service or lower quality (full planes, no late-night flights).[6] We saw this effect in another guise in Chapter 4: Price collusion in an unregulated industry diverts rivalry into nonprice forms of competition.

The problems of regulatory decision include making the right decision in the first place, as well as motivating the regulated firms to respond with the desired allocation decisions. Suppose that the Federal Energy Regulatory Commission set

[5]For other examples see A. E. Kahn, *The Economics of Regulation: Principles and Institutions* (Cambridge, MA: MIT Press, 1988), Vol. II, pp. 49–59.

[6]R. E. Caves, *Air Transport and Its Regulators* (Cambridge, MA: Harvard University Press, 1962), Chap. 14; George W. Douglas and James C. Miller, III, *Economic Regulation of Domestic Air Transport* (Washington, DC: Brookings Institution, 1974).

itself the task of determining the best price for natural gas under economic criteria for the efficient use of resources. Because natural gas is a fixed stock available within the earth's crust, its appropriate price at any one time depends on the demands expected to prevail for it in all future times (because the gas used now cannot be used later). The commission could hardly secure the data and perform the necessary analysis, and be able to convince the courts (if its decision were appealed) that it had employed a fair and objective procedure. Regulatory agencies not infrequently are asked to make decisions that require more analytical capacity than they possess, or that depend on data that do not exist in any objective form.[7]

Even the requirements of legal procedure have proved an important liability of regulation. Cumbersome procedures mean that a long time elapses between when an issue starts through the regulatory mill and when it comes out the other end. Procedural delays (with a boost from political mechanisms) interacted with rapid inflation during the 1970s to cause many regulated prices to be set too low. Consider the electric utilities. During the 1960s they experienced rapid productivity gains from new large-scale generating equipment, so that the electricity prices sanctioned by the regulators were yielding increasing profits. Occasionally a regulatory agency would demand a rate cut, or a utility would even propose one itself. But by the late 1960s inflation began to outrun productivity gains, so the utilities lined up to request rate increases. As inflation accelerated, by the time a utility got one rate-hike request through the commission the new rates still yielded below-normal profits.[8] The regulators understood the problem, but also recognized that political entrepreneurs would quickly intervene on behalf of inflation-wracked consumers if the commission added to their woes.

### Effects of Regulation

We began this chapter by suggesting that direct regulation of business for securing satisfactory market performance is an alternative to putting our trust in competitive processes (under the watchful eye of the antitrust authorities). When we weigh the effects of regulation, therefore, we need to know, not how regulated industries perform in some absolute sense, but whether they do better or worse when unregulated and with competitive processes at work. Economists have done a good deal of research on the regulated industries, and their findings are by and large pessimistic about the ability of regulation to improve performance.

Market performance must be evaluated industry by industry, and we shall inspect a few of the regulated industries. Electric power companies come close to meeting the structural criteria for natural monopoly, and we might expect their market performance to be better under regulation if any sector's is. It has been

[7]For a study of these constraints on a regulatory decision, see M. E. Porter and J. F. Sagansky, "Information, Politics, and Economic Analysis: The Regulatory Decision Process in the Air Freight Cases," *Public Policy*, Vol. XXIV (Spring 1976), pp. 263–307.

[8]Paul L. Joskow, "Inflation and Environmental Concern: Structural Change in the Process of Public Utility Price Regulation," *Journal of Law and Economics*, Vol. XVII (October 1974), pp. 291–327.

possible to examine this question by comparing the performance of electric utilities between regulating and nonregulating states, because not all states adopted regulation at the same time. Some, but not all, studies indicate that regulated utilities earned lower profits and charged lower prices than unregulated ones before the late 1960s.[9] Since then, the evidence suggests that regulation has depressed prices below the utilities' costs, a result of inflation and lags in regulatory procedure. They were earning about 4 percent when the real cost of equity capital is about 7 percent; they were therefore forced to postpone investment to cut costs and meet future demands for electric power.

In the 1980s the utilities sought various ways out of this bind. They embraced the idea of buying power from independent generators (the regulators had to allow the costs of these purchases to be covered by the utilities' revenues) and got regulators to let them bribe large customers to make energy-saving investments. The resulting allocations are not obviously efficient.

Should electric power be pushed onto the deregulation bandwagon? Economists are doubtful that deregulation can be very useful. Local distribution systems remain natural monopolies, so their deregulation is out of the question. What might be feasible is to detach electricity-generating plants from the distribution networks, creating an arm's-length wholesale market in which regulated distribution systems bid for power supplies from unregulated generating firms. But such a wholesale market would not necessarily perform well. A given distributor would face moderately concentrated sellers, so that the old problem of monopoly would probably arise. Furthermore, power is consumed and produced at the same instant, and it is not obvious that market signals can optimally assure that all demands at each moment are served by the most efficient set of supplying facilities.[10]

Air transport is another sector in which performance under regulation received close scrutiny, and we now have the confirming evidence of actual deregulation. The main effect of regulation was to keep fares on popular and densely traveled routes higher than they needed to be. But the airlines did not skim any excess profits from these revenues, partly because of the adjustment of nonprice competition. Regulation imposed other inefficiencies. It locked airlines into historical patterns of routes connecting various cities, although these route structures should have been redrawn as commercial aircraft went through their rapid evolution. The coming of deregulation freed existing airlines to expand into new routes, bringing more competition to the individual city-pair markets and letting the carriers rationalize their operations. New carriers entered with lower fares than the formerly regulated firms whose employees (it turned out) had captured substantial profits in the form of above-market wages. As a result, fares in the larger markets fell sharply relative to the airlines' operating costs. The median fare was 100 percent of a fare

[9]Robert H. Smiley and William H. Greene, "Determinants of the Effectiveness of Public Utility Regulation," *Resources and Energy*, Vol. V (March 1983), pp. 65–81.

[10]Paul L. Joskow and Richard Schmalensee, *Markets for Power* (Cambridge, MA: MIT Press, 1983).

norm used by the Civil Aeronautics Board in 1975, before deregulation, but by 1980 it had fallen to 73 percent of that norm (adjusted to 1980 costs).[11]

> When the airlines were deregulated, economists thought that entry barriers were low and competition would work well. Lately, however, the tables have been turned, as the airlines devised policies that (although generally cost-efficient themselves) sharply raise entry barriers and concentration. The hub-and-spoke organization of routes tends to blockade entry by other carriers into the hub city. In congested airports the incumbent airlines have gained control over scarce boarding gates. The computerized reservation systems give advantages to the airlines that control them. Frequent-flyer plans induce regular travelers to be loyal to established airlines and shun newcomers. Although few economists believe that these changes warrant a return to regulation, they predict that allocative efficiency will be poorer than was hoped.

The market structure of the highway truck transportation industry is quite free from natural monopoly. It has limited scale economies, low capital intensity, easy entry, complete mobility of companies from one geographic market to another, no product differentiation, and so on. In fact its structure largely matches the classic requirements for pure competition. One is not surprised that trucks came under regulation in the 1930s largely because their shipping rates were undercutting those of the regulated railroads. We expect regulation to worsen performance, and it did. The Interstate Commerce Commission restricted trucking companies to carrying limited ranges of commodities along specified routes, often precluding them from serving intermediate points or forcing them to travel by roundabout routes. For the same reasons, they often made backhauls empty. These requirements increased the industry's costs well above the minimum attainable. Deregulation of trucking began in 1978 and was confirmed by legislation in 1980. By 1983 the real price of truckload shipments had fallen by 25 percent, smaller shipments by 11 percent. There is no evidence that service to smaller communities has deteriorated—one consequence of deregulation that some had feared. The 1980 legislation also deregulated many competing railroad rates. Although railroads and trucks compete for the business of shippers, their regulatory distortions were quite different. Railroads' profits were too low, and their capacities (especially little-used branch lines) were too large. They needed to contract their operations, rationalize their pricing, and improve the quality of their service. Those tasks have proceeded.[12]

## The "New" Regulation and Industrial Organization

The "new," or social, regulation, risen since the 1960s, has less to do with the organization of markets than did the old regulation. We can nominate market failures that explain the public's decision to install this regulation. The regulation

---

[11]Elizabeth E. Bailey, Daniel R. Graham, and Daniel P. Kaplan, *Deregulating the Airlines* (Cambridge, MA: MIT Press, 1985).

[12]Clifford Winston et al., *The Economic Effects of Surface Freight Deregulation* (Washington: Brookings Institution, 1990).

of environmental pollution (Environmental Protection Agency) and vehicle safety (Department of Transportation) rests on "external diseconomies." The plant that dumps polluting wastes into a river takes no account of the cost or disutility they impose on people living downstream; the driver of an unsafe vehicle may reckon the chances he takes with his own well-being but give no heed to people whom he may injure in an accident. Another market failure behind some of the new regulation is that of costly and "impacted" information. The consumer has no easy and cheap means to weigh the safety of the household appliance or prescription drug that she purchases, and the manufacturer does not necessarily want to level with her on the risks it involves. The Consumer Product Safety Commission issues standards on the design, construction, performance, and other such characteristics of many consumer products, and the Food and Drug Administration (FDA) regulates the introduction of new drugs.

These economic explanations for the new regulation—if indeed they are the right ones—do not draw directly on the models used in this book. (Compare the concept of "natural monopoly.") But the new regulation does interact with market structures, and so our apparatus helps us to understand its causes and consequences. Take the FDA's responsibility for approving new drugs. The FDA supervises the whole process of testing a new drug, first on animals, then on human subjects, to ensure that it is safe and causes no excessive side effects. Since 1962 the FDA has also determined the *efficacy* of a drug, demanding proof that it is not just safe but also really has the positive benefits claimed for it. Public policy in effect substitutes regulation for product differentiation and its problems, as described in Chapter 2. The public (physicians and patients both) are ill-equipped to evaluate a drug short of actually using it. One solution is for drug makers to stand behind their trademarks, differentiating their products by putting their reputations on the line. The user who cannot judge a drug's safety and efficacy then takes the maker's advertising and trademark as a signal of the drug's quality. The FDA's approval procedure then might be a way around this indirect "signal" process, the disappointments it may bring to consumers, and the advertising and sales-promotion resources that it uses.

Concepts of market structure also help to analyze the effects of the new regulation. The FDA's testing procedures both delay the development of new drugs and increase the costs and risks facing pharmaceutical manufacturers. Most researchers have concluded that FDA regulation has contributed to slowing down the rate of introduction of new drugs, which now often become available in other countries long before they may be used in the United States. The costly and risky approval procedure also is changing the structure of the pharmaceutical market. Because of the increased risk, a drug maker benefits from being large enough to pursue a portfolio of products. The large firm can more likely spread the heavy costs of a project that fails to win approval over others that do.[13] In 1984 the Waxman-Hatch Act relieved subsequent entrants into the production of a drug of repeating the

---

[13]See Henry G. Grabowski, *Drug Regulation and Innovation: Empirical Evidence and Policy Options* (Washington, DC: American Enterprise Institute, 1976).

same onerous testing that was required of its innovator. The change means that, once an innovator's patent expires, effective competition arrives more quickly than before (although still not quickly, because of the goodwill retained by the innovator).

The same concentrating effects on market structures flow from regulation of industrial pollution. The strategy employed to clean up the environment has concentrated on requiring companies to change the technology of their production processes in order to stop or drastically reduce their pollution of air and water. The technology of pollution abatement, it turns out, is usually very capital-intensive and subject to economies of scale. Therefore pollution control increases the average unit costs of all plants, but those of small plants proportionally more than large ones. Whether the industry is initially competitive or oligopolistic, pollution abatement will cause its product's price to rise, demand to decline, and some plants (and firms, presumably) to exit from the industry. The small units tend to go first, and so seller concentration becomes higher than before—perhaps significantly higher.[14]

## PUBLIC ENTERPRISE

If antitrust policy is not always adequate, and direct regulation has difficulty commanding good market performance, why not nationalize? Public enterprise has long been a matter of acrimonious debate over the general principles of "socialism versus capitalism." But the challenge to capitalism, especially one coming from the Marxist camp, has usually been based on considerations of personal income distribution and on relationships of socioeconomic power within the society, not on economic performance in particular markets for goods and services. Here our concern is with market performance. What can we expect from public enterprise? And what do we actually get?

A casual student of the American economy might suppose that public enterprise is a purely academic question in this bastion of capitalism. Yet public enterprises are important in key sectors of the economy—the postal service, water and sewer services, local transportation and local gas and electric utilities in many urban areas, the Tennessee Valley Authority, and for a time Conrail in the railroad sector. Indeed, about 15 percent of employment in the United States is in the public sector (all government employment, not just government business enterprises), more than in some other industrial countries. In the 1980s the tides did not favor public enterprises. Just as deregulation was prominent in the United States, the privatization of public enterprises proceeded vigorously in other countries. The process of privatization flushed out much information on how public enterprises performed.[15]

---

[14]Robert A. Leone, ed., *Environmental Controls: The Impact on Industry* (Lexington, MA: Lexington Books, D. C. Heath, 1976).

[15]The process is particularly well documented for Great Britain. See John Vickers and George Yarrow, *Privatization: An Economic Analysis* (Cambridge, MA: MIT Press, 1988), and R. E. Caves, "Lessons from Privatization in Britain," *Journal of Economic Behavior and Organization*, Vol. XIII (March 1990), pp. 145–169.

Before the wave of privatizations, public enterprises were distributed about the same way among sectors of the Western industrial economies, despite a great deal of diversity. They were common in sectors producing what people perceive as the "necessities" of life—water, electricity, and so on. They remain common in sectors whose outputs involve external economies or diseconomies—broadcasting, coal mining. They are used for large-scale and risky ventures, such as crude-oil exploration and development and nuclear energy. Like direct regulation, they appear in industries subject to clashing minority interests—railroads, coal mining. And among manufacturing industries in the European countries, they turn up in the older capital-intensive industries, especially those marked by large-size companies. This list offers some echoes of the explanations advanced earlier for the sectors chosen by the public for direct regulation—market failure, interest-group conflict, and the like.

### Behavior of Public Enterprises

In order to study public enterprises, we need a framework for thinking about how they might behave. They are generally organized much as private businesses are, except that the government holds their equity capital. These equity shares may not exist as pieces of paper, but the government nonetheless takes on the role of equity holder, because it must make up any losses that the public enterprise runs and can appropriate its surpluses if it chooses. The public enterprise may get some instruction from the government about its policies but usually enjoys a large measure of independence.

If the management of the public enterprise is told only to "serve the public interest," it may enjoy a good deal of discretion about what objectives to follow. Like the large private company whose shareholders are widely dispersed (see Chapter 1), its managers may heed their own preferences in deciding how to run the company. One plausible preference that has been suggested is to maximize the public enterprise's chances for survival and its independence from outside interference. That simple postulate allows us to develop some predictions about how public enterprises might behave. Consider these questions:

1. What profit rate would a public enterprise seek to earn? A business in the public sector surely gains political support from its customers by offering its goods and services at lower prices. Therefore we would not expect to find the public enterprise earning excess profits, because these could be traded away for political support. But by the same token we would not expect the enterprise to run sustained losses. These would force it to go to the government for financial help, and this would surely compromise its independence. The firm therefore should tend to seek a normal rate of profit. Public enterprises indeed seldom seem to earn excess profits unless they have been organized as instruments of taxation (state liquor stores in the United States, tobacco monopolies in France and Japan). Public enterprises do sometimes run substantial losses, but often with the predicted consequence that the

government tires of the subsidy and lays down tighter operating rules for the management. Many European public enterprises for years sought to earn no interest on the capital they received from the government, but governments eventually recognized that this capital has an opportunity cost, and forced their enterprises to justify its use by earning interest.

2. Would a public enterprise undertake price discrimination? The answer to this depends on how the enterprise's political support is affected by its relations with various groups of customers. We expect it to charge higher prices to nonvoters than to voters; for example, a local electrical utility might charge higher prices to any customers that are located in another political jurisdiction. But there is a reason for expecting that public enterprises will avoid charging people different prices and use simple pricing structures, thereby discriminating in favor of the customer groups it costs more to serve. Charging everybody the same price sounds fair, and this improves political support. Besides, should the cost of serving a particular group of customers fall, the enterprise can probably wring the most extra political support from this development by spreading the benefit among its various groups of customers. The post office charges no more for delivering a letter to a remote rural location than to a city address, though the former's cost is much higher.

3. Would a public enterprise minimize its costs? It would like to achieve the lowest possible costs, because any cost reductions can be passed on to buy more political support from customers. However, this conclusion no longer holds if payments for inputs are a source of political support. The employees of the public enterprise are voters and may represent a strong interest group as well, and paying higher than market wages could gain their political support. As the European countries came to suffer high unemployment rates in the 1970s, many of their public enterprises grew quite tolerant of inflated payrolls. Domestic manufacturers of inputs used by the public enterprise can provide political support, whereas foreign manufacturers cannot, and so we would expect public enterprises to pass up imported inputs even when they are cheaper. This preference for domestic suppliers has greatly inflated costs for some European airlines and telecommunications companies.

These predictions contain mixed implications for the performance of public enterprises. We would not expect a public enterprise to behave as a monopolist except when selling to a group with no political power, although it may charge too low a price for its product and thus employ too many resources. The public enterprise's disinclination to use price discrimination is another bright spot, up to a point; however, public enterprises also tend to charge customers who are costly to serve the same prices as those who are cheap to serve, and that is itself a form of price discrimination. Finally, the enterprise may trade off low input costs to get political support.[16]

[16]The ideas presented in this section were developed by Baldwin, *The Regulatory Agency*, Part II; and Sam Peltzman, "Pricing in Public and Private Enterprises: Electric Utilities in the United States," *Journal of Law and Economics*, Vol. XIV (April 1971), pp. 109–148.

This simple model of the behavior of the public enterprise may strike you as either too cynical or not cynical enough. Why should we not simply assume that public enterprises will do the best for the general economic welfare? On the other hand, why should we not just conclude that government is less efficient than private business because the profit motive is absent? A point of our analysis is to show that the attitudes (of the political left and right, respectively) behind these questions are seriously oversimplified. Serving the general economic welfare is not an operational goal for a public-enterprise manager operating in an interest-group environment, a fact tacitly recognized in the arrangements typically made to insulate public enterprises from the self-seeking pressures of "day-to-day politics." Likewise, if the profit incentive for efficiency does not bear continuously on the public enterprise management, it also does not pervade the incentives of the management of a large company with market power and widely dispersed stockholders. Thus, our simple approach may be less simplistic than its intellectual competitors.

### Performance of Public Enterprises

Does public enterprise perform better than private companies would, carrying out the same activity under direct regulation? Better than private companies under the antitrust laws? We need the answers to these questions in order to make the best choice of public policies. Unfortunately, they are very difficult to secure. The considerable literature on public enterprises, especially those outside the United States, conveys the impression of enormous diversity. Public enterprises often operate in market situations that contain elements of "natural monopoly," and so they can act in a variety of ways within the limits set by market forces. Their behavior shows the imprint of whatever historical circumstances led to their creation or nationalization. Finally, they reflect the political traditions and governmental institutions of the country in which they operate. The following generalizations are therefore highly tentative.[17]

The public enterprises that appear to display the best records are those carrying out activities particularly subject to natural monopoly and market failure. The French national electricity authority, Electricité de France, gets good marks for the technical sophistication of its planning and for its pricing practices. Also, it has realized the advantages of an integrated national grid of interconnected power sources, a task that was made more complicated for the United States power industry by the fragmentation sustained and in some ways enforced by regulation. Another example is Britain's National Coal Board, which faced the task of reducing the

---

[17]The following studies are helpful, in addition to those already cited: William G. Shepherd et al., *Public Enterprise: Economic Analysis in Theory and Practice* (Lexington, MA: Lexington Books, D. C. Heath, 1976), Part II; Chris Harlow, *Innovation and Productivity under Nationalisation* (London: George Allen and Unwin, 1977). A. E. Boardman and A. R. Vining, "Ownership and Performance in Competitive Environments: A Comparison of the Performance of Private, Mixed, and State-Owned Enterprises," *Journal of Law and Economics*, Vol. XXXII (April 1989), pp. 1–33.

number of the industry's old and inefficient underground coal mines and minimizing the human cost of the miners put out of work.

A more mixed picture is displayed by the large public industrial enterprises that operate in manufacturing industries, competing with oligopolistic rivals. These are found chiefly in the petroleum, automobile, steel, and chemical industries. Some have been highly venturesome and willing to take large risks, and good records for product and technical innovation are not uncommon. However, dominant public enterprises have also put too many innovative eggs in one basket, often betting on one technology and putting competing ones out of the running. There are clear-cut cases of conglomerate empire-building for no evident public purpose. And the public oligopolists have usually been highly cooperative with their private-sector competitors, promoting or at least cooperating with cartel arrangements and using the government's power to stave off import competition. The lack of competitive effectiveness is in some cases due to the public firm's having relatively higher costs than its private rivals (because it is, for instance, prevented from discharging redundant workers), and public enterprises have generally been less profitable than their private competitors. In the 1970s the losses run by public enterprises became increasing irritants to their governments and set the scene for privatization, especially in Britain.

What is the best public policy for getting good market performance? The one safe statement seems to be that no method is best for all market structures and political environments. Perhaps in the future we will be able to use data on market structure not only to predict an industry's performance but also to foretell in what policy environment it will deliver the best performance possible.

## SUMMARY

Companies in some industries are subject to direct regulation of their prices and other terms of sale, and of entry into their industries. Federal, state, and local governments undertake such regulation. Direct regulation may have resulted because the public perceived that market performance was poor in "natural monopoly" situations, where the antitrust laws were no help. But regulation has also come about to resolve political conflicts through cross-subsidy or simply to benefit organized interest groups (the industry itself, or its customers or other affected voters). Regulatory decision making runs into problems of providing the correct incentives for regulated firms. When companies are allowed to earn a rate of profit expressed as a percentage of their invested capital, they have an incentive to use too much capital. Also, the regulation of prices in a competitive industry like air transport can cause the regulated firms to enter into inefficient nonprice competition.

Economists' appraisals of the effects of direct regulation have been rather negative. It may have reduced monopoly profits in "natural monopoly" sectors, like electric power, but technical efficiency seems to have suffered in the process. In more competitive sectors, such as air transport and highway truck transportation, the costs of technical inefficiency have been very high indeed, and the gains from restricting monopoly or reducing other deficiencies in performance are probably negligible.

The "new," or social, regulation (health, safety, environment, and the like) deals with the problems of market failure not closely connected to industrial organization. However, its consequences include effects on market structure—increasing seller concentration, in some cases.

Placing enterprises in the public sector is another possible method of securing improved market performance. In the Western industrial countries we find public enterprises chiefly in the public-utility industries and in the large-scale and capital-intensive manufacturing industries. Public enterprises usually enjoy a good deal of independence from their governments and are given only general instructions about how to conduct their affairs. In those circumstances they might be expected to maximize their political support and survival prospects. To do this they would tend to earn normal profits (excess profits can be used to buy political support from customers with lower prices; subnormal profits bring political interference). They would minimize costs unless the terms on which they buy their inputs affect their political support; but they may buy support by paying high wages to their workers and favoring inefficient domestic suppliers over efficient foreign ones.

The performance of actual public enterprises in the United States and abroad is too diverse to allow easy generalizations. Abroad, the public enterprises with the best records seem to be those in "natural monopoly" situations, such as electric power, and those dealing with problems of external economies or diseconomies. Public enterprises in the European manufacturing industries have generally not been positive forces for securing competitive market performance, although some of them have been efficient and innovative. Many public enterprises were privatized abroad during the 1980s, just as many regulated sectors were at least partly deregulated in the United States in the 1970s.

Ideally, we would be able to predict scientifically from knowledge of an industry's market structure whether it would perform better under direct regulation, as a public enterprise, or as a private business under the general antitrust laws. Although we have indications, the day of a confident prediction lies in the future.

# Selected Readings

The following three undergraduate textbooks extend the framework of analysis presented in this book and summarize much more of economists' research on industrial organization: F. M. Scherer and David Ross, *Industrial Market Structure and Economic Performance*, 3rd ed. (Boston: Houghton Mifflin, 1990); Douglas F. Greer, *Industrial Organization and Public Policy*, 2nd ed. (New York: Macmillan, 1984); and Dennis W. Carlton and Jeffrey M. Perloff, *Modern Industrial Organization* (New York: Harper Collins, 1989). An advanced textbook on the theoretical aspects of the subject is Michael Waterson, *Economic Theory of the Industry* (Cambridge, England: Cambridge University Press, 1984).

Volumes that address business motives and their effects on business behavior and the economy are John Kenneth Galbraith, *The New Industrial State*, 4th ed. (Boston: Houghton Mifflin, 1985); Gordon Donaldson and Jay W. Lorsch, *Decision Making at the Top* (New York: Basic Books, 1983); and John R. Meyer and James M. Gustafson, eds., *The U.S. Business Corporation: An Institution in Transition* (Cambridge, MA: Ballinger, 1988).

Some older studies of basic elements of market structure remain useful. See Joe S. Bain, *Barriers to New Competition* (Cambridge, MA: Harvard University Press, 1956); Basil S. Yamey, ed., *Economics of Industrial Structure* (Harmondsworth, England: Penguin, 1973); Robert T. Masson and P. David Qualls, eds., *Essays on Industrial Organization in Honor of Joe S. Bain* (Cambridge, MA: Ballinger, 1976); Joseph E. Stiglitz and G. Frank Mathewson, eds., *New Develop-

*ments in the Analysis of Market Structure* (Cambridge, MA: MIT Press, 1986); and P. A. Geroski, *Market Dynamics and Entry* (Oxford, England: Blackwell, 1991).

Integration in the large enterprise is examined historically by Alfred D. Chandler, *The Visible Hand: The Managerial Revolution in American Business* (Cambridge, MA: Harvard University Press, 1977); and analytically by Oliver E. Williamson, *The Economic Institutions of Capitalism* (New York: Free Press, 1985), and Dennis C. Mueller, *The Corporation: Growth, Diversification and Mergers* (Chur, Switzerland: Harwood Academic, 1987).

The best general descriptions of patterns of market conduct are found in textbooks such as Scherer and Ross, Chaps. 7–10, and Greer, Chaps. 11–16. On conduct with commitment, see Marvin B. Lieberman and David B. Montgomery, "First-Mover Advantages," *Strategic Management Journal*, Vol. IX (1988), pp. 41–58, and Pankaj Ghemawat, *Commitment: The Dynamic of Strategy* (New York: Free Press, 1991).

On mergers, see the symposium of papers in *Journal of Economic Perspectives*, Vol. II (Winter 1988). Market conduct is discussed from the viewpoint of the business decision maker by Michael E. Porter, *Competitive Strategy: Techniques for Analyzing Industries and Competitors* (New York: Free Press, 1980).

Studies of individual industries furnish one of our most valuable sources of knowledge about industrial organization. Highly readable chapter-length industry studies are provided by Walter Adams, ed., *The Structure of American Industry*, 8th ed. (New York: Macmillan, 1990), and Leonard W. Weiss, *Case Studies in American Industry*, 3rd ed. (New York: Wiley, 1980). Three of the more successful book-length industry studies are Lawrence J. White, *The Automobile Industry Since 1945* (Cambridge, MA: Harvard University Press, 1971); Gerald W. Brock, *The U.S. Computer Industry: A Study of Market Power* (Cambridge, MA: Ballinger, 1975); and John A. Stuckey, *Vertical Integration and Joint Ventures in the Aluminum Industry* (Cambridge, MA: Harvard University Press, 1983).

For lively debates on some of the determinants of market performance, see Harvey J. Goldschmid et al., eds., *Industrial Concentration: The New Learning* (Boston: Little, Brown, 1974). Research and innovation are considered broadly by Christopher Freeman, *The Economics of Industrial Innovation*, 2nd ed. (Cambridge, MA: MIT Press, 1982). The statistical evidence on market performance is summarized by John S. Cubbin, *Market Structure and Performance— The Empirical Research* (Chur, Switzerland: Harwood Academic, 1988).

Textbooks on "government and business" discuss government policies toward promoting or restricting competition. See William G. Shepherd, *Public Policies Toward Business*, 7th ed. (Homewood, IL: Richard D. Irwin, 1985). Antitrust cases are excerpted and analyzed by Don E. Waldman, *The Economics of Antitrust: Cases and Analysis* (Boston: Little, Brown, 1986). Recent issues are addressed by John E. Kwoka, Jr., and Lawrence J. White, eds., *The Antitrust Revolution* (Glenview, IL: Scott Foresman, 1989).

A reprinted classic study of regulation is Alfred E. Kahn, *The Economics of Regulation: Principles and Institutions* (Cambridge, MA: MIT Press, 1988). Many interesting volumes deal with regulation and deregulation. They include: Elizabeth E. Bailey, David R. Graham, and Daniel P. Kaplan, *Deregulating the Airlines* (Cambridge, MA: MIT Press, 1985); Clifford Winston et al., *The Economic Effects of Surface Freight Deregulation* (Washington: Brookings Institution, 1990); S. P. Bradley and J. A. Hausman, eds., *Future Competition in Telecommunications* (Boston: Harvard Business School Press, 1989); and James Q. Wilson, ed., *The Politics of Regulation* (New York: Basic Books, 1980). Richard Schmalensee, *The Control of Natural Monopolies* (Lexington, MA: D. C. Heath, 1979), provides an analytical treatment of natural monopoly and its regulation.

For studies of public enterprise, see John Vickers and George Yarrow, *Privatization: An Economic Analysis* (Cambridge, MA: MIT Press, 1988); and Ingo Vogelsang, *Public Enterprise in Monopolistic and Oligopolistic Industries* (Chur, Switzerland: Harwood Academic, 1990).

Many of the articles on industrial organization in the professional journals are too technical for undergraduate consumption, but the following journals do publish papers that are both substantial and reasonably accessible: *Journal of Industrial Economics*, *International Journal of Industrial Organization*, *Journal of Law and Economics*, *Journal of Economic Behavior and Organization*, *Review of Economics and Statistics*, and *Antitrust Bulletin*.

# Index